PROMOTE THE DOG SITTER

Promote the Dog Sitter

AND OTHER PRINCIPLES FOR

LEADING DURING DISASTERS

Edward L. Conley

LIONCREST
PUBLISHING

PROMOTE THE DOG SITTER
And Other Principles for Leading during Disasters

FIRST EDITION

ISBN   978-1-5445-3414-5 *Hardcover*
      978-1-5445-3415-2 *Paperback*
      978-1-5445-3416-9 *Ebook*

For Jordan, Shea, Jake, and Jiw. Thanks for leaving the light on.

Contents

Introduction

We stood with our hearts thumping in front of deployment decider Agnes Mavercek, who sat behind her desk.

"I see you speak Spanish," she said, scanning her finger down my résumé, which actually said I had *studied* Spanish five years before. It wasn't a question, so I didn't correct her.

On my right was Steve Pratt. We had joined FEMA on the same day three months earlier, along with twenty-two others. Our official titles were Emergency Management Specialists Trainees, but everyone called us "interns" at FEMA headquarters on 500 C St. SW in Washington, DC.

At that point, Steve's and my FEMA careers had been a mild disappointment. No one knew quite what to do with us. There had been a few floods during the summer, but none of the disaster veterans wanted inexperienced, know-nothing novices stumbling around their field operation.

We were late-twenties, low-on-the-pay-scale rookies. Steve was twenty-seven, and I was twenty-nine; both of us were married with kids. We knew FEMA represented our last chance to have a calling. Our families had sacrificed a lot when we'd quit our old jobs, chased our dreams, and relocated to DC to join the agency. Now, we were too broke and had too many personal obligations to start over again if this emergency management thing didn't work out.

Hurricane Hugo represented a career-altering opportunity. The monster storm slammed the US Virgin Islands, followed by a direct hit to Puerto Rico. Hugo then turned northwest for a few days before barreling into Charleston, South Carolina. Still not done, Hugo continued churning north, walloping North Carolina. The storm caused so much devastation that the World Meteorological Organization retired the name Hugo.

In 1989, Hugo became the biggest disaster in FEMA's then-ten-year history, and the agency wasn't meeting public expectations. The media was firing criticisms, and members of Congress were calling for investigations. The field teams just knew they needed more help.

Out of staff, headquarters scoured the hallways to find available personnel. As we later found out, Steve and I weren't an easy sell despite the shortage.

"Really?" the Puerto Rico staff asked. "You're sending us two interns?"

"Don't worry, at least they speak Spanish," FEMA headquarters tried to reassure them.

"Okay," said Agnes. "Get some per diem money. Go home, pack your bags. Catch the first flight to San Juan."

It was time for us to find out if the disaster response business was meant for us, and if we were meant for it.

I stayed in Puerto Rico for three months and with FEMA for another twenty-seven years. I think it worked out for both of us. (If you're wondering, Steve remained working in the industry for decades, too.)

WIND MET RAGE AND RAIN, AND TOGETHER THEY BECAME A STORM

When I started my emergency management career, I didn't know policies, programs, or procedures. I didn't speak the emergency management language. Words flowed from my mouth less like a river than like a stagnant lake clogged with debris.

The only thing I had going for me was that I loved being involved with emergency management.

I was always fascinated by the weather. One of my earliest childhood memories was standing in the street gutter next to my mom, watching swirling dark clouds above wind-blown trees. In elementary school, I even won a prize in a poetry contest for my disaster sonnet:

Wind met rage and rain, and together they became a storm. (Give me a break, I was just a kid.)

I joined FEMA six months short of my thirtieth birthday. Before that, I had tended bar, worked on the Ski Patrol, and sold advertising space in newspapers. Starting over at twenty-nine, with student loans, no savings, and a wife and two kids, was tough.

My previous job paid me $35,000 a year in 1989. FEMA offered me $16,000 a year to start.

The only way for me to get more experience (and make more money) was to go on a disaster deployment, which meant leaving my family for months. I knew deployments came with the job. I accepted that and was excited by the opportunity.

However, I worried about being fired. I worried about being relegated to the back seat. I was super sensitive about being dissed because of my age or title. Even after finishing my training and becoming an emergency management specialist, some still called me "the intern."

I was also the type of person who couldn't shake off small mistakes. I agonized over mispronouncing a word or using the wrong one in the presence of agency leaders. I would replay what I said in my mind at night and sometimes for days. I thought no one would forget my mistakes. Once, I tried to praise an agency director for building robust regional offices. Instead of "strong regions," I said, "strong regencies." That bugged me for months.

I struggled with the politics of working in a government job and office. I had to learn to balance personal beliefs with my professional responsibilities. And this was before social media. Now it seems like anything you share on your Facebook or Instagram account has the potential to be connected back to your organization. There's a lot less privacy for people joining the force today than when I started.

I also struggled with whom I owed my professional loyalty to, when to speak up, and when to keep my mouth shut. I lacked confidence in sharing my observations, even though some of them turned out to be good. I particularly sucked at articulating my thoughts in meetings.

If you picked up this book, my guess is that you have some of these challenges, too.

By the time I retired from FEMA in 2016, I had worked more disasters and been deployed in the field longer than practically anyone in the agency's history to that point. Counting my winters on the Ski Patrol, I've spent three decades responding to incidents. I've been an emergency medical provider, intern, logistics courier, and recovery center manager. On occasion, FEMA selected me for special assignments, like a city liaison, but mostly, I was an External Affairs Officer (EAO).

An EAO has a seat at the command table and works with all elements of the disaster response. Emergency public information is considered an operational resource during a crisis, so EAOs are trained to think and act like incident responders. EAOs are deployed for every event, usually when things are most chaotic in the first wave. My position gave me an excuse to wander into rooms while crisis leaders decided what to do. As you read my stories and wonder how I happened to be there, that's the answer.

What I learned has shaped me, forming the drive to write this book. I wanted to share these stories because perhaps they will help you too.

THE CRISIS LEADER FUTURE GENERATIONS CAN COUNT ON

Someone once asked what I remembered most after three decades of being a disaster responder. My answer wasn't a specific event, like Hurricane Katrina or 9/11. It was this: When you work in emergency management, you go to work when something bad happens, but what sticks with you is all the good you see. You meet the most incredible people and see the best in them. You take a small part of that and keep it inside. You carry it to the next disaster, and it becomes part of who you are.

What I remember most are the people I worked with, those I worked for, those who prepared, and those who survived. People from both the response and survivor sides taught me how to do my job—people who made a difference in the recovery of their family, neighborhood, community, tribe, city, state, territory, or nation. They came in all ages, races, genders, and backgrounds, but they all had one thing in common: leadership principles.

I have repeatedly found that leadership is the single most crucial component of any crisis. It's more important than money, helicopters, sirens, and cots. Outstanding leadership expands partnerships, improves teamwork, and overcomes challenges, leading to less suffering, faster help, and more robust and resilient communities.

Let me predict a few things that will happen during your career: you'll get seated next to the disaster conspiracy theorist at a family reunion; almost every incident notification call will come when you're out of the office; and your generation will crave accountable and authentic crisis leadership.

Whether you are an emergency coordinator, specialist, trainee, volunteer, disaster reservist, or intern at the beginning of your career, I wrote this book with you in mind. You will discover the principles used by people who were at their best when things were the worst. They are the principles for becoming a crisis leader that future generations can count on.

This book is not theoretical. It's not academic. It's a book for practitioners written by a practitioner who was in the "eye of the storm." While it includes stories about leaders who failed (and why), it is mostly about leaders who succeeded (and how). Ideally, it complements the training you will receive, including the established doctrine, response and recovery frameworks, and incident management systems you already know and use.

To complete a thought by Scottish historian Niall Ferguson, "We are constantly teetering on the edge of chaos," so we might as well be connoisseurs of the experience.

Are you ready to become a bold, compassionate, and wise crisis leader? I hope so. The world could use a few more.

It all begins with Principle Number One: Show Up.

CHAPTER 1

Show Up

HOW TO BE SEEN ON SCENE

"Better three hours too soon than three minutes too late."

—WILLIAM SHAKESPEARE

Representatives from response organizations arrive at the scene to set up an interagency coordination center following a disaster in Colorado. Photo by Michael Rieger/FEMA.

I saw the message waiting on my phone and knew what it meant: Vacation over. Deployment on. Hurricane Katrina was waiting on line one.

I had spotted the story on sidewalk stands a few days earlier. The front page of every newspaper announced that Tropical Storm Katrina had crossed the southern tip of Florida and entered the warm Gulf waters. Favorable conditions for hurricane development, reports said. I'd felt my disaster antenna twitch at this news. Maybe it was New Orleans' turn.

It shouldn't be that bad, I told myself. I wasn't in the current rotation. I wouldn't get a call unless it was all-hands-on-deck, and what were the odds of that?

The phone message was from Cindy Ramsey, one of the Federal Emergency Management Agency's top officials. "I don't know where the hell you are, but you need to call me. FEMA director Mike Brown has canceled your leave. The levees are breaking. All hell's breaking loose. And the governor won't come out of her mansion."

It was *all-hands-on-deck*. I crisscrossed the room, stuffing clothes in my bag as I called Cindy back.

"It's bad," she said when we connected. "I need you to start in Houston. We'll bring you to Louisiana later. Harris County Judge Robert Eckels is opening the Houston Reliant Center for the Katrina evacuees. Go there. Meet him. Hard to track you down. No one knew where you were."

"I know," I said. "Sorry. I'll go to Houston. But you need to know—"

"Is Andrea with you?" she interrupted, referring to Andrea Booher, a well-known documentary photographer who worked on assignment for FEMA.

"She is."

"Tell her Houston, too, for now."

"Okay, but I need to tell you something."

"Later," she said, "I've got to go. We can talk when you get to Houston."

"That's what I need to tell you. It might take a few days."

"What? Why? Wait, where are you?"

"Spain," I said. "... Hello? Cindy? Are you still there?"

"Get moving," she finally said. "Get back here as fast as you can. You know what to do. Show up in Houston."

Within minutes, Andrea and I had our bags packed. We jumped in our rental car, and I drove to Madrid Airport as she worked the phone with Continental Airlines to arrange flights.

"We'll get you there," the Continental customer service representative said. "But hurry. Your first flight departs soon."

On the highway outside of Madrid, federal police pulled us over for a vehicle search at a drug and alcohol checkpoint. I was sure my frantic look and sweat-drenched brow contributed to them motioning us to the side. No way to catch our flight now, I thought.

"Huracán. Los Estados Unidos," quick-thinking Andrea explained, flashing her FEMA badge. They waved us through. The disaster must have been a monster. It seemed the whole world already knew about it.

We ran through airports and sat fidgeting through fifteen hours of plane flights with nothing to do but wait. It was every emergency manager's worst frustration: not being where they're needed.

Thirty-six hours after I talked to Cindy, we stood in the parking lot at the Houston Reliant Center. Plenty of challenges lay ahead—for me, the agency I worked for, and most of all, the communities hit by Hurricane Katrina.

But we had crossed at least one hurdle. We showed up.

DISASTER RESPONSE IS NOT A SPECTATOR SPORT

All aspiring emergency managers need to learn the principle of showing up, which means arriving on the disaster scene ready to help. This principle should be self-evident. The only way to learn how to manage emergencies is by throwing yourself into them.

What's more, showing up defines you as a crisis leader. It becomes part of your legacy. Any discussion about you, your career, and what you might have accomplished begins with stories about the disasters you worked on and the things you did in person.

Emergency managers do a lot besides responding to disasters. They develop exercises and plans, conduct training, manage funds, handle critical administrative requirements, and build new Emergency Operations Centers (EOCs). All of these tasks are essential to ensuring a robust crisis response. Yet policy leaders, legislators, influential outsiders, and the public will judge you only by how they perceived you handled the last disaster.

You can be a great planner, and no one will know. You can have excellent employee morale-boosting events, and no one will care. You can implement a worthwhile and impactful preparedness campaign, and everyone will forget. When people talk about FEMA, they speak about Katrina, Maria, COVID-19, or 9/11. They don't talk about the new carpet in the operations center.

This chapter will define what we mean by showing up and why it's essential to make it one of your core emergency management principles.

WHAT DO WE MEAN BY SHOWING UP?

FEMA gives certificates for each disaster employee's work. The top two federal and state leaders running the operation sign them. These certificates mean a lot to the people who get them. Some employees tape theirs to their office walls. I saved every one of mine. They are necessary because of what they represent:

- **You were physically on the scene.** You left your office and deployed to the disaster. You walked the rubble and saw the impact firsthand.
- **You engaged with people outside your organization.** For me, showing up meant talking with more people outside of my organization than inside it.
- **You contributed to the response.** Your position or title is not essential. What mattered was that you had a disaster assignment. Showing up can mean something different depending on whom you ask. Yet, for everyone, there is one final test: *When things got ugly, did I answer the call?*

IMAGINE A DISASTER WHERE NO ONE SHOWED UP TO HELP

Of course, that will never happen. Yet, in my experience, there were never enough people who did, and this problem has the potential to get worse. According to FEMA's Daily Operations Briefing, within the agency, daily cadre availability for immediate deployment in the first three months of 2022 often hovered below 25 percent, partly because many staff were already assigned elsewhere.

Across the industry, more than 70 percent of emergency management specialists are older than forty, according to Zippia career demographics in 2022. The field needs a pipeline of new professionals ready to replace those retiring in the coming decades. The necessity for crisis leaders is also growing as disasters become broader in scope due to population growth in high-risk areas, emerging infectious diseases, the rise of violent extremism and terrorism, and impacts associated with climate change.

Not every emergency manager in the nation needs to be on the scene for a three-county flood in rural Ohio. Yet everyone who works in emergency management needs to show up some of the time and be ready all the time.

New emergency managers will often try to emulate the office all-star. The one who projects in-the-office confidence, walks the right way, and knows how to act around superiors. Yet when disaster strikes, this is often the person who disappears, at least in my experience.

When I first started with FEMA, division bosses encouraged my incoming management trainee class to admire a fast-rising young program manager. After watching him for a few weeks, I could see why. He displayed a good game. I remember how he would tilt his head and lean into the conversation when talking with agency leaders. He had perfected the purposeful walk.

But there's a reason we refer to the "Showing Up" principle and not the "Showing Off" principle.

We quickly discovered he was an Eddie Haskell, the iconic duplicitous character from the 1960s television sitcom, *Leave It to Beaver*. He couldn't have been more condescending to new employees away from supervisors. The most extended conversation I ever had with him was when he told me, "Goddamn it, watch where you're walking" when, klutz that I am, I almost spilled coffee on his new, bright white tennis shoes.

In a quarter-century of disaster work, I saw him twice in the field. Once during Hurricane Andrew, he popped into the Miami office for a few days. The second time I saw him at an after-action meeting following a Midwest flood event. He was an office all-star, a leadership pet, and a crisis no-show. You'll meet a few of those in your career. As you may have already discovered, when the bell rings not everyone shows up, despite the expectation that disaster duty is a job requirement. We'll examine different reasons for this in more depth later in the chapter.

Make sure you're looking to someone worthy of your admiration, not the Eddie Haskell of the office that leadership told you to look toward. Mentors are great when you start, but pick someone you've seen in action—and still admire—in an actual crisis.

Look for responders who have weathered the criticism that comes with this type of career without losing their enthusiasm for the job. Are they quick to scramble out of the office before the hurricanes hit? When you talk with them, are they eager to explain their passion for what they do? If you want to learn how to make "showing up" one of your principles, you want to pick someone like that.

You are just as likely to receive criticism and unsolicited analysis as you are unadulterated praise. There will always be sideline observers, ivory-tower critics, and generic blowhards happy to tell you what you should have done. Yet you will never see them on the scene getting their hands dirty. If you take nothing else away from this chapter, focus on the mission, your job, and the people you serve—because that's what those who embrace the "Showing Up" principle do.

If you're reading this, I'm confident you entered this line of work for the right reasons. You want to help people and make a difference for your community, state, and country. I can hear you say, "I want to work on disasters. That's why I got a job in emergency management." You didn't pick up this book to learn how not to be a crisis leader. You may also see these stories as an opportunity for professional growth.

You want to be the type of crisis leader people can count on. That means you need to make showing up—the *right* way—one of your core principles. Develop the habit early and continue to practice it throughout your career.

When I worked on disasters, and things got crazy, I'd often hear crisis leadership say, "Call John or Jane. That's who we need, and they'll show up." You want to be the John or Jane they mean.

THE FOUR COMPONENTS OF SHOWING UP

Showing up is more than dropping into the Emergency Operations Center and saying, "Here I am." That counts, to a degree, but there's more to this principle. You must:

1. Recognize your opportunity and responsibilities.
2. Deal with your fears.
3. Decide what type of emergency manager you want to be.
4. Be prepared.

OPPORTUNITIES AND RESPONSIBILITIES

Chris Luhring was a twenty-nine-year-old police chief and rookie emergency manager in Parkersburg, Iowa, when an EF5 tornado struck on May 25, 2008. It was the first EF5 recorded in Iowa in more than thirty years. "It was like an atomic bomb got dropped on our city," he said.

"Sure, it was my job to respond, but it was more than that," Chris recalls. "I grew up in Parkersburg. I knew everyone. I saw the city grow and prosper. I was new to my job and not the most confident guy. But the first thing I told myself was, 'This was the day you were born for.'"

Like Chris, you might be brand new to your position when a historic disaster gets dropped in your lap. There will be no warm-up. Ready or not, you have to show up.

More likely for newcomers, months or years will go by where your only action will be training, exercises, and more training. You may even feel embarrassed telling people you work in emergency management but have never managed an emergency.

In my case, I experienced the combination of both extensive training and not having managed an emergency yet. As I mentioned in the introduction, not long after starting with FEMA in 1989, I deployed to Puerto Rico for Hurricane Hugo. Then it was three years before I worked on another disaster when, in 1992, the agency sent me to south Florida for Hurricane Andrew.

Though both were major disasters that needed engagement from throughout the federal government, I wasn't anywhere near the first wave out the door. I had to beg for a chance to go. Yet those deployments were how I found my calling. They made me realize I wanted to be on the scene when disasters occurred.

Between those assignments, I continuously asked for deployments and was left out. Meanwhile, colleagues decades older than me with hundreds of disasters under their belts were running disaster operations in different areas of the country—several supported disasters on remote islands in the Western Pacific and the Marshall Islands. To a thirty-one-year-old aspiring emergency manager, it sounded unbelievably cool.

I saw the pride they felt working with state, territorial, and local officials, helping people overcome difficulties, and rebuilding damaged infrastructure. I wanted to be like them: a part of disaster history. Though I had a job in the profession, I still felt like an observer, watching others handle the catastrophes. I believed I had the right tools and mentality. I just needed the chance to prove it.

In 1993, I received a transfer from the grant and training side of FEMA to the disaster response side. No longer a replacement player, I was now on the first team out the door. Even better, my new boss was John Swanson.

Within the emergency management world, John Swanson was a legend. For decades, he had been the go-to guy in FEMA, the one you called when the big ones hit. After years of struggling for more opportunities, I'd now be getting them on John's team. I had it made.

Yet while I had physically moved into that role, it took time to make the mental adjustment. Inside, I was still the guy who had to beg for a deployment. Even in a disaster responder position, I still thought I needed an invitation when disaster hit.

Not long after joining John's team, floods slammed the Midwest.

They started in May, and by July, nine states and five hundred counties from Minnesota to Missouri had been declared disaster areas by President Bill Clinton. It was later named The Great Midwest Floods of 1993. This historical event marked a transformational moment in my career, though I was slow to see it coming.

One afternoon, I was on vacation in California, splashing in the pool with my kids, when John called.

"How's your vacation going?" he asked. He still made me nervous. Preoccupied with what to say next, I missed the sarcasm.

"Umm. Okay. How are you doing?"

"We're on the move. South Dakota's getting it now." Then John stopped talking.

He was not the kind of boss to explain himself. It was starting to hit me by this point, though I had not completed the mental one-eighty.

"Flooding pretty bad, huh?" I asked.

"That's right."

"Do you want me to go?"

"Well, that's kind of why we hired you."

"I'll be there tomorrow."

And there it was. I was no longer the last guy left in the office.

Now I was being requested. It took four years, but the door had opened.

It's a pretty significant shift when you come off the bench. First, you're waiting for your chance. Then, when your time finally comes, you can't believe it.

If you're wondering when yours will happen, my guess is sooner rather than later. As I previously mentioned, disasters are getting worse and more frequent, while the impacts of climate change loom ever more significantly. Yet timing is not your only concern. There's also an emotional aspect to showing up.

DEALING WITH FEARS

It's normal to feel nervous when something important is at stake. As soon as I had the opportunity—I had been working toward it for so long—my mind played a cruel trick. It said that if I showed up, I wouldn't meet the expectations of my colleagues.

It took a decade of responding to different disasters before I felt fully confident showing up to the scene. Veteran crisis specialists will tell you this is normal.

It takes time to experience a gamut of incidents. And it takes time in the field to understand the cycle of mitigation/preparedness/response/recovery phases, to see the scope of challenges communities face during their recovery years, and to grasp the intent of all the programs. At least it did for me.

For many, the fear of underperforming never goes away. That's because few careers carry as much pressure and expectation as emergency management. That fear is not an entirely negative emotion, either. It keeps you on your toes, for sure. However, you can't allow the fear of underperforming to prevent you from showing up.

I watched many career emergency managers avoid deployments over the years. To me, it was apparent that something scared them about working in the field. From what I have seen, when disaster professionals can't overcome their fears, it often plays out in one of two ways:

1. They invent excuses not to show up.
2. They try to talk the boss out of allowing them an opportunity to show up.

INVENTING EXCUSES

I have seen high-ranking government officials find an excuse not to answer every time the phone rang for them. Yet these are people whose job description says: help communities after a disaster.

Why the disconnect? I suspect some were worried about being exposed as less capable than their position, title, or reputation suggested. Perhaps they felt expectations for the response were too high, or their involvement would result in failure. There are legitimate reasons why someone would not be available for deployment. However, being afraid to do the job isn't one of them.

TALKING YOURSELF OUT OF AN OPPORTUNITY

In the movie *Remember the Titans* (2000), the star quarterback gets hurt, and the coach calls for the second-string quarterback, who says that he's not ready and can't make all the plays.

"Yes, you can," the coach tells Ronnie. "Your team needs you tonight. You're the Colonel, and you're going to command your troops!"

Many people worry about being overlooked or underestimated in their work. Yet when an opportunity comes, they talk themselves out of accepting it. Having selected hundreds of people for disaster assignments, I often reassured talented people that they could do their jobs. And in every case, they exceeded my expectations.

I also can't recall a single instance where a crisis leader I admired threw an employee into a situation to fail. They offered assignments that turned out to be exciting and challenging. When a respected disaster pro gives you a job that's more than you think you can handle, take it. That usually means they've realized your potential before you have. Something about disaster works draws out the best in people, which means you are capable of much more than you think.

HOW TO OVERCOME YOUR FEARS OF SHOWING UP

It can be scary stepping into a disaster knowing that someone's well being—or livelihood—may depend on you. Yet if you find reasons not to show up early in your career, it will only get harder to start later. Remember that feeling unprepared is normal. You must learn to manage your hesitancy when disaster strikes.

It helps to realize what it means to get *the call*. While others are evacuating the disaster area, you get called in. During a pivotal moment for your organization, community, tribe, state, or country, you were essential enough to be asked to help. You also won't be showing up alone. Committed and compassionate professionals will surround you with one common goal: to help the people and communities impacted.

In addition, you may get lucky.

In 2002, Guam was hit by two typhoons. Typhoon Chataan struck in July. The second, Super Typhoon Pongsona, clobbered the island territory in December. According to the NOAA-funded Pacific Regional Sciences and Assessment Program, one severe tropical storm threatens Guam every year.

At Guam Memorial Hospital following Pongsona, doctors delivered babies and performed surgeries with flashlights because the facility had no power.

A few months later, Governor Felix Camacho embarked on an international trip to tout the island's recovery and encourage tourists to return to beachfront hotels. However, Guam Memorial Hospital CEO Dr. David L.G. Shimizu had a different message about visiting Guam.

"Come to Guam, and you may get lucky," he told us. When asked what he meant by that, he said, "It's only when you are faced with a disaster that you begin to learn what you are made of. You may think you know, but it's only by going through one that you will truly know."

WHAT TYPE OF EMERGENCY MANAGER DO YOU WANT TO BE?

Showing up defines the type of responder you will be, sometimes for your entire career. Emergency managers plan, prepare, and train for disasters, but not everyone wants to be at the scene when the bell rings.

Are there roles in emergency management that don't require you to show up on the scene every time? Of course. There also are many opportunities to be a vital part of the disaster team but in a secondary role. You might get assigned to a regional coordination center.

Yet, on some occasions, you need to show up. You need to be on the scene. It's the only way to round out your knowledge and skill set. To fully grasp the impact of your agency's policies, programs, and public communications, you need firsthand experience delivering them when people need them most. What's more, the emergency management community will define you by how you handle deployment moments when they arise. When family, friends, and colleagues reflect on your emergency management career, guess what they'll remember most? All the disasters you worked.

FOUR WAYS TO SHOW UP ON A DISASTER

When you work in emergency management, there are four ways to handle a deployment request and a disaster assignment opportunity:

1. Don't show up.
2. Pretend to show up (also called disaster tourists).

3. Show up unprepared.
4. Show up to make a difference.

Now let's examine each of these in turn.

Those Who Don't Show Up

I once worked with a high-ranking official who managed to get out of every field assignment in his decade-long career. Every time a disaster hit, he would have a death in the family, a wedding, a child's college enrollment trip, or a medical appointment.

He did a fine job in the day-to-day non-crisis setting, but when things got bad, he was never there. I suspected that he initially turned down opportunities because he lacked program knowledge and wasn't confident he could represent the agency publicly. Later, I believe he feared being exposed as an imposter when he was further along in his career.

The agency learned never to count on him when the disaster occurred, which was a burden for those trying to staff the incident. On the other hand, by not showing up, he created opportunities for aspiring emergency management specialists ready to take his place.

At the beginning of your career, you need to establish yourself as someone who shows up. If you become known as someone the organization can't count on, they'll stop asking, which will make it nearly impossible to build that reputation later. Showing up often involves making more personal sacrifices when you're younger and starting a family. That can be tough, but it will give you more flexibility to say "no" later in your career.

Pretending to Show Up (Also Called Disaster Tourists)

The second type of responders are those who pretend to show up. They dash in for a few days or a week so that they can put the disaster on their résumés. They won't even have an assignment. They just hang around taking up space, resources, and time.

"You only have a finite amount of energy [as a leader during crises]," former Atlanta mayor Keisha Lance Bottoms told Harvard T.H. Chan School of Public Health's Mary Bassett during the 2020 COVID-19 response. "It takes a lot to pretend."

Following one large-scale incident, federal and state agencies established tent-filled campsites as lodging for out-of-the-area responders. A few top leaders spent some nights at the camp before departing the disaster completely, to say they had "shared" in the experience. Yet it was nothing compared to actual responders who lived in the tents for months. It was distracting for the response because it required extra logistical arrangements. Some relief staff felt the visit belittled those working to help disaster survivors.

Those Who Show Up Unprepared

It's equally distracting for responders when new arrivals ask for things like maps, a place where they can gas up their car, and if they can borrow a flashlight, hard hat, or masks. It's incredibly frustrating because it's clear they haven't read the Incident Action Plan or situation reports before arriving. When you show up, show up prepared. That means doing things yourself, not asking other responders to take time away from their jobs to help you.

As with most responders who have had a lot of deployments

away from home, more often than not, I was able to secure adequate lodging before I arrived on the scene. I also experienced disasters where I shared a room in a busted-up hotel with no power, though, or slept on an office floor at an Emergency Operations Center (EOC), or spent a few nights camping in my car. Part of your job is to be ready to support the disaster before the disaster overhead team is ready to support you.

Whenever I scheduled hiring interviews at FEMA, I always gave prospective employees sufficient directions to find our regional headquarters, but not step-by-step. The test: Could they find the office using other sources, show up on time, and be ready to talk? This expectation is not unlike typical deployment instructions responders receive, which often lack specific details. One interviewee arrived twenty minutes late, frazzled and furious at me because he couldn't find my office. He didn't get the job.

Those Who Show Up Ready to Make a Difference

As a young man, my dad served in the Korean War. Shortly before he died, he shared his admiration for General Matthew B. Ridgway.

"Before Ridgway took over, we had commanders who didn't care how many of us got killed as long as all the rear echelon officers got their promotions," my dad told me. "Ridgway came to the front lines. He'd stand beside you, looking through his binoculars. He'd say, 'Tell me what you see. What's happening out there? What do you think we need to do?'"

If you're trying to gauge whether someone is showing up for the right reasons, here are a few things to look for:

- They aspire to make a difference.
- They want to develop expertise and experience by working the crisis.
- They want the responsibility.
- They are building credibility to influence change and advance initiatives, such as the mitigation programs James Lee Witt institutionalized when he ran FEMA in the 1990s.
- They believe the best way to become a good leader is by working through a crisis side-by-side with people you admire.

ALWAYS BE PREPARED

I once attended a FEMA training class solely focused on packing for a disaster. My favorite lessons: 1. Roll your clothes up instead of folding them to save room. 2. Pack your clothes in two bags. If you lose one, you can still go to work.

Veteran responders usually have their tips for being prepared, often based on experience gained from painful lessons. Some are standard, like having essential safety gear such as a flashlight. Others are unique to the individual. One responder always brings a ten-dollar roll of quarters. "You'll be amazed at all the times this still comes in handy," she said. "Laundry, for one."

Despite varying approaches, all responders share the same goal for arriving prepared: do everything you can to be self-sufficient. You owe it to the operation to come as prepared as possible and not burden the impacted community. Arriving prepared includes:

- packing the correct type of clothes and boots;
- having the necessary work-related equipment;

- educating yourself about the incident and the community impacted;
- being certified in First Aid and CPR;
- getting immunizations (CDC recommendations for disaster responders include Tetanus and Hepatitis A and B, for example; and
- using your resourcefulness and capabilities to take care of yourself.

Part of always being prepared is also self-training before deployment. I spent excessive time watching disasters unfold in different parts of the country and the world. I imagined myself on the ground, evaluated their priorities, and monitored their tactics. It's a great way to pick up insights that'll become part of your response tool kit.

DO WHAT IT TAKES TO SHOW UP

Sometimes your first challenge is not the disaster itself but getting there. It's the nature of this business that a catastrophe always seems to come when it's least convenient: during a vacation, on top of the holidays, or when you're already dealing with another disaster.

While it would be great if the stars aligned to help whenever disaster strikes, great emergency management specialists have to think on their feet and find a way to show up.

Hours after the terrorist attacks on 9/11, a Tuesday, my public affairs team in Colorado received a call from FEMA's Bri Rodriguez. She told us to get to New York City as fast as possible and run media operations for the federal search and rescue teams arriving at Ground Zero.

That was the entire deployment order. We had to figure out how to get there. The FAA grounded all commercial air travel as a result of the attacks. It was agonizing to have the assignment, watch the disaster unfold on TV, but be stuck 1,778 miles away.

In a stroke of ingenuity, one of our employees, Luisa Rivera, connected with Preston Robert Tisch, the owner of the New York Giants, who was also stranded in Denver. He had attended the September 10th Monday Night Football game between his club and the Denver Broncos.

Luisa arranged to designate Tisch's private jet as an emergency relief flight. In exchange for the designation, which allowed him to fly home, Tisch gave us four seats on his plane for our FEMA public affairs crew: videographer Jim Chesnutt, photographer Andrea Booher, Brett Hansard, and myself. We flew into New York on September 12 with Tisch and several officials from the National Football League.

LEGITIMATE ABSENCES

There are times when you legitimately can't show up. That's okay. I always tried to honor time-off requests from long-time employees drawn away by family obligations while working for FEMA. If a disaster hit, I wouldn't call them. Inevitably, however, they would call *me*.

"Why didn't you call me?" they'd ask.

"You told me you weren't available."

"I'm not, but you still could have called."

It's a strange feeling that many in the profession share. Even when you can't go, you still want the call. You fear your organization will determine you're replaceable—that you've been forgotten. Yet everyone needs a break. What's more, you should never show up when you'll be distracted by personal issues. It's neither fair to the operation, nor a job requirement, to show up physically but not mentally.

Don't think the operation will fail if you don't go. Some federal responders opted out of 9/11 early on because they didn't feel safe, which was understandable.

There will always be more disasters. If you miss one, it won't be your last chance. When you legitimately can't deploy, be honest about your reasons. Family needs, a physical ailment, or mental exhaustion are all acceptable reasons not to show up.

DEVELOPING THE SHOW UP PERSONALITY

When I study emergency management professionals who have the show up personality, I notice four things:

1. They use a unique emergency management vocabulary.
2. They "wish" for an opportunity to prove themselves and help people.
3. They support first responders by having a first responder mindset.
4. They always remember what it means to work in emergency management.

Let me explain what I'm talking about.

THE EMERGENCY MANAGEMENT VOCABULARY

Every profession has a language, words unique to their industry, that only insiders get. Emergency management is no different.

The Weather Channel, for instance, becomes *My Employment Channel* or *My Travel Channel*. Other examples:

- There's disaster time and the time between disasters that some responders referred to as "peacetime."
- "What do you do in real life?" (meaning, What do you do when you're not working disasters?)
- You use "hit" instead of impact to describe where the disaster struck.
- You understand the "Waffle House Index," coined by former FEMA Administrator Craig Fugate. The index is used as one indicator of how a community may be faring immediately after a disaster and is based on the chain's reputation for being disaster prepared. "If you get there and the Waffle House is closed? That's really bad," Fugate told *The Wall Street Journal* in 2011.
- And the "Jim Cantore Index." If Cantore (The Weather Channel meteorologist) is doing live updates from a location near you, buckle up.

Also learn the unique vocabulary of the community to where you deploy. Once a FEMA auditor based in a big city came to check how Kim Lee, the local emergency manager in Fremont County, Wyoming, had spent his federal preparedness grant.

"I was working on a project outside of town when the auditor arrived," said Lee. "I told him to wait for me at the first cattle guard down the highway."

The auditor never showed. When Lee returned to his office, he had a message.

"The auditor said he drove up and down the highway for hours," Lee said, "and he never could find that guy guarding the cattle."

WISHING FOR DISASTER?

You may find yourself wishing for disaster and wonder if that's okay. Many emergency managers describe the adrenaline rush when a disaster threatens. Psychologists say that emotional reaction is similar to feeling excited, even happy. If you've had this experience, you may have wondered if it's a bad thing. It's not.

It doesn't mean you wish bad things to happen to people. You're acknowledging that bad things can happen, and you want to be there to help when they do. After all, the next disaster is not a matter of if, but when.

When you have this emotional response, it indicates you want to be part of the team rushing to help. You want to do your job. That's what wishing for a disaster means: wishing for a chance to help a community.

"That's because you don't work in the disaster business because you have to. You do this job because you love to," according to Ambassador Dr. Jacqueline McBride-Jones, a veteran crisis responder and emergency management thought leader.

So, if you find yourself wishing for a disaster and thinking you're not normal, don't worry. You're normal.

ARE YOU A FIRST RESPONDER?

Not long after I retired from FEMA, I helped a recent college graduate apply for a reservist position with the agency. After FEMA hired him, I gave him some of my extra Personal Protective Equipment (PPE), including a hard hat, a yellow safety vest, waterproof pouches, safety goggles, flashlights, and gloves.

When he finished his week-long orientation training at FEMA's Emergency Management Institute, he called me and offered to return the gear.

"Why?" I asked.

"They said I don't need it. I'm not a first responder," he said.

Bosses and training officers have told me I *was not* a first responder throughout my FEMA career, while others have told me I most certainly *was.*

There are two reasons trainers—mainly at the federal and state level—tell the emergency management newcomers they are not first responders. First, some consider it disrespectful to first responders who perform life-saving missions—firefighters, police officers, doctors, nurses, medical technicians, and search and rescue specialists. Second, some government officials don't trust what emergency management specialists will do if given the title of first responder. They think newly-minted hires will treat the designation like a James Bond-type license to respond and start performing duties beyond their expertise, as if they've suddenly been authorized to drive fire trucks. (Okay, this did happen—*once.*)

However, I believe emergency management specialists who arrive during the response phase of an incident need to consider themselves first responders. I'm sure we all agree it's incumbent on every emergency manager to stay within the boundaries of their own role and expertise and to stay outside of others'.

However, labeling responders from the emergency management community as first responders doesn't disrespect the lifesavers. It shows respect for them. Emergency management specialists who arrive on the scene need to be as prepared as possible. They need to avoid being a burden on the response and becoming another casualty for the impacted community.

Maybe if we start telling new emergency management specialists they may find themselves as part of the first response, they'll show up personally prepared with some basic PPE, which might actually come in handy. Most responder deaths occur after the initial incident when people let down their guard. Earthquakes have aftershocks, extended power outages are common, floods often follow wildfires, and all disasters have unexpected consequences.

Furthermore, emergency management professionals need to practice what they preach. The federal government spends enormous amounts of money each year encouraging American families to prepare. Official messages warn people they may be on their own for up to ten days and to stockpile appropriately. We ask individuals to help those around them who need assistance after disasters. In other words, we expect the public to be first responders within the scope of their capabilities and knowledge. Shouldn't the emergency management community follow the same advice?

"If you're talking about a sudden, large-scale disaster, there will never be enough professional first responders right when they're needed," Natalie Simpson, an Associate Professor of Operations and Management and Strategy at the University of Buffalo, said in a 2019 report issued by the Arizona State University Walter Cronkite School of Journalism. "Everybody is a first responder."

You are a first responder if you're on the front lines representing your organization during the response phase of a crisis. It doesn't matter whether you're driving a transit bus during an evacuation, working at a pharmacy during a pandemic, organizing your family's finances after a flood, deploying to another jurisdiction as part of a state-to-state mutual aid agreement, or coming in for FEMA. You're part of the disaster first response team at that moment.

Ricardo Zuniga, "Zuni," is a FEMA external affairs officer who has been embedded with life-saving missions at the front end of large-scale disasters, including search and rescue efforts and body recovery details. "In those assignments," he said, "I arrived ready to support, including matching the gear and clothing of the teams I got assigned to. I did this out of respect for them, to make sure they didn't have to worry about my safety or find protective equipment for me, and to make sure I could hit the ground ready to work."

Some of the best emergency managers are those who have either worked as a life-saving responder or attended some formal first response training, such as the National Wildfire Coordinating Group S-190 Introduction to Wildland Fire Behavior. They know how to stay in their lane, support other response elements, arrive prepared, and remain safety-conscious.

Here's my recommendation: when you work in emergency management, you need to be ready to consider yourself a first responder. Because when you show up in the response phase, that's who you'll be.

REMEMBERING WHAT IT MEANS TO WORK IN EMERGENCY MANAGEMENT

When remembering what propelled them to this business, many emergency managers recall a personal experience when some-one showed up for them. I love hearing these stories.

"When I was seven," said Dr. McBride-Jones, "I got caught in floodwaters in Cumberland County, New Jersey. My dad appeared out of nowhere. He lifted me. He moved me to higher ground. It inspired me to be the type of person who could show up and help lift people up as my dad did.

"Never underestimate what can happen after you show up and show you care," said McBride. "Show up. Just show up."

When you show up, you become a part of history. It may be the history of famous disasters that future generations read about in books and watch on film. It may be history that communities hold only in their memories, or that families recall with their stories, but it is history nonetheless.

No matter the role you play or the prestige of your title, no matter how long you stayed on scene, that history includes you. You were part of the response. You will always be part of that response. Because you showed up.

CHAPTER 2

Step Up

HOW TO MAKE A POSITIVE ATTITUDE YOUR CALLING CARD

"Perpetual Optimism Is a Force Multiplier"

—COLIN L. POWELL

FEMA Community Relations teams responded to a string of tornadoes that hit the Southern States in the late 1990s. Photo by Andrea Booher/FEMA.

In the aftermath of Haiti's catastrophic earthquake, the US Embassy in Port-au-Prince held an outdoor multidenominational service. Gathering amid almost total devastation and with a growing sense of desperation among the earthquake's survivors, the chaplain issued an inspiring call to action to the nearly 100 people in attendance—but with a twist.

He wanted to be out digging in the rubble, too, trying to free those who might still be trapped, but that would be wrong for him. He said that was not his job and would just be getting in the way. Then he asked everyone to remember their jobs and think about how they could best help. He said 'every job, no matter how small, [would] help build a foundation for Haiti's recovery and [would] make us all part of the same team digging in the rubble.'

COURTESY OF BRETT HANSARD, GOVERNMENT TECHNOLOGY/EMERGENCY MANAGEMENT

I was in the audience that day, and that's how the chaplain's message resonated with me. You step up by doing your job, not someone else's. Most of all, you step up with your attitude. No one arrives at a crisis fully trained for every contingency, but what the response needs most is not your expertise. In every disaster, there will come a time when leadership looks around and says, we need everyone to step up. When that happens, you should be ready to do your part.

PICTURE THE DISASTER SCENE

Think about all the places you might go after you get the call. It might be an on-scene command post or an incident staging area. Maybe you see yourself deployed to an evacuation center.

Think about the environment. Make it chaotic. Now, ask yourself three questions.

1. What type of leadership inspires me?
2. What sort of team attitude do I want in the room?
3. What kind of attitude will I bring to the scene?

By 2022, Tammy Littrell was one of the highest-ranking officials in emergency management. I first worked with her years earlier when she ran FEMA's Information Technology (IT) shop in Denver. Whenever I went to her with computer issues, her response was, "Thanks for letting me know. We need to fix that right away. Your job is too important. You need to be able to communicate." She was never frustrated when I brought her a problem and seemed keen to fix it. She also acknowledged my work, which made me feel good, like what I did mattered.

The ancient Chinese proverb of Yin and Yang interweaves contradictory opposites, such as crisis equals disaster and opportunity. Emergency managers say the same thing with three words: "I got it." Learning the value of bringing a can-do attitude will lead to many more leadership opportunities.

There are several things you can do to bring a positive attitude to every disaster. Here are five ways to demonstrate that you "got it."

1. Bury the ego.
2. Step up by being prepared.
3. Learn how to talk to disaster survivors.
4. Study history.
5. Become a crisis optimist.

Let's go further in-depth on each point.

BURY THE EGO

One of the best ways to positively contribute to any disaster operation is to learn how to bury your ego. Forget thinking or pretending you have all the answers—you don't. This advice may sound counterintuitive, but you'll gain respect and credibility when you admit you're stuck or overwhelmed during a disaster. Admitting vulnerability demonstrates that you've put the mission ahead of your ego. Being honest creates trusting teams and galvanizes resources for the simple reason that emergency managers like to help each other out.

Big egos generate a negative vibe in any operation. Too much effort goes into shoring up their insecurities. Thinking back on the annoying egomaniacs I worked with, it seemed they spent much time criticizing other people and different organizations. They should have spent more time identifying unmet needs and being honest about their lack of capabilities. They tend to say "I" instead of "we" and like to point out how you and your team screwed things up.

As former FEMA administrator Craig Fugate liked to say, "The disaster is not about you." Forget about publicity, your rank, your parking spot, the size of your office, or who is to blame. In a crisis, your objective should be solving problems, meeting lifesaving and life-sustaining needs, implementing recovery programs, and remaining survivor-centric. You can't do that alone. And you can't pretend to do it, either.

Instead, Ask for Help

Years ago, a state emergency management director became notorious for waiting too long to ask for help. The state he oversaw suffered for years from damaging floods. Each spring, as the water began to rise, FEMA would check in with his office: "Hey, do you need us yet?"

"No, we're okay," they would say.

A week later, FEMA would call again. "We're watching the news and reading situation reports. Are you sure you don't need our team?"

"Nope, we're fine," they would say again.

This back and forth would repeat for weeks. Then, we got the phone call everyone expected at the last minute: "Where the hell are you guys?" By then, it was often too late.

No one thinks less of leaders who ask for assistance in crisis management. It takes poise to admit that you cannot handle everything yourself. What's more, leaders who ask for help tend to view the ask as an opportunity to expand the team and leverage resources and technical expertise. People often think asking for help signals they cannot do their job, which ironically causes relief efforts to falter. Asking for help in a crisis does not make you weak. It means you are ready to lead.

Chris Luhring, who, following his time as emergency manager, became city administrator for Parkersburg, Iowa, described the thought process this way:

"After our (2008) tornado, my early concern was the morgue:

- I wanted it dignified so that families wouldn't be embarrassed.
- I needed it to be large enough to handle the estimated fatalities.
- I needed help. I had no morgue training."

"When I do presentations," Luhring said, "One of my favorite lessons is: You don't need to know everything post-disaster. But you do need to know who knows what you need to know."

As Chris emphasized, disaster relief is a team effort. Successful leaders establish connections that foster coordination and sharing of information. They respect the responsibilities, legal authority, and capabilities of other entities. They build interagency teams to access specialized skills and set common priorities.

Also, They Focus on Building Long-Term Positive Relationships

Fragile egos worry more about protecting their reputation than sharing credit. For them, the disaster is all about me, me, me. They want to say "I did it," not "we did it." Unless something goes wrong, of course. Then they say, "I didn't do it. You did."

Influential leaders publicly recognize the contributions of other people. They stick with their team members and provide confidence to take risks. They are also forgiving.

We all lose our cool sometimes, and frustration often boils during disasters. It's rare for disagreements to turn into career feuds. People who work on disasters share an esprit de corps. Yet, implementing operations can have unexpected tests that are temporarily infuriating. The point to remember is not how to win disagreements but how to end them.

It's hard to imagine disasters with more tense moments than 9/11, where I ran the federal external affairs office in New York during the first two months of the response. The terrorist attacks killed 2,763 people in New York City.

Approximately ten days after the attacks, one of Mayor Giuliani's Public Information Officers (PIO) called my hotel room around midnight, livid. A federal search team member had interviewed with radio station 1010 WINS and described finding large numbers of bodies in the Twin Towers rubble and the emotional toll it was taking on the search teams.

FEMA had violated its agreement with the city. When Giuliani's office agreed to allow FEMA photo and video crews twenty-four-hour access to the World Trade Center disaster site, they had established two rules. The first was not to release images to the media of the deceased. The second was that no federal responder was authorized to talk publicly about finding human remains. Only city officials had the authority to speak on the subject.

I supported the policy wholeheartedly. More than two thousand people remained missing. Families were desperate to know what had happened to their loved ones. City leaders wanted grieving family members treated with respect. Vague announcements from unofficial sources about finding bodies at Ground Zero helped no one.

There was also still hope. Though it turned out the final survivor of the attacks was rescued in the early afternoon on September 12, people thought there was a chance more survivors remained in pockets beneath the rubble ten days into the search.

"It's more than hope for us," a FEMA Urban Search and Rescue team member from Sacramento told me during the search. "Every day we go out to The Pile, we believe we'll find survivors. That belief drives us."

"Call the station and kill the fucking interview," the PIO screamed. "I swear to God, we're going to kick every federal rescue worker out of Ground Zero and send them home. I don't know what the hell authority your spokespeople think they have. Why would they talk about this? Why would they do this to people?"

After he hung up on me, I called the 1010 WINS news director. I told him calmly that the federal responder did not have the authority to speak on the subject of body recovery. Furthermore, the interview had damaged the federal government's relationship with the City of New York. The station agreed to take the soundbites off the air.

I called the PIO back. "Thanks," he grumbled. Then his tone lightened. "Hey. Someday, you and me, let's get drunk."

With that, he gained my respect and loyalty forever. When people get upset with you during a disaster, deal with the frustration but maintain the personal relationship. You can often become closer to someone after a disagreement than before it.

STEP UP BY BEING PREPARED

In chapter one, we covered the importance of *showing up* prepared. Yet that responsibility doesn't end when you sign in. It goes beyond ensuring that you don't wade through flooded streets or report to debris-strewn areas wearing tennis shoes. Stepping up with a positive attitude means always thinking about how your actions affect others. This includes:

- Read each Incident Action Plan (IAP). Then roll it up and stick it in your back pocket or throw it in your backpack. You'll be amazed by how many questions you'll get asked each day that can be answered by referring to the IAP.
- Learn how to BLUF—Bottom Line, Up Front. Make the subject line of emails relevant, and say if you expect action or a response back. Think twice before hitting reply-all to any emails you receive. Acknowledge receipt of essential emails so the sender doesn't worry whether you received the information. It's about respecting others' time.
- Buy a cellphone rain pouch and keep it around your neck. It is your most valuable tool during a crisis. I'm embarrassed to admit I've ruined many cell phones by dropping them in oceans, rivers, and toilets. Protect your primary form of communicating.

If you do only these three things, you'll end up making a contribution to every disaster.

LEARN HOW TO TALK WITH DISASTER SURVIVORS

Sometimes you think you know everything about a person based on their reputation. Then you meet them in a crisis, and it turns out you knew nothing at all.

During a 2007 flood in Westchester County, New York, then-Senator Hillary Clinton toured a damaged neighborhood with FEMA Director R. David Paulison, a seasoned responder. The former fire chief for the Miami-Dade Fire Rescue Department, Paulison knew how to walk through the rubble, talk to survivors, and handle those situations with dignity and respect. Clinton had a reputation for being cautious and not very friendly. Commentators labeled her a micromanager of her political outings, preferring scripted events.

Several area politicians joined Clinton and Paulison on tour. Most of them had a first-time-on-a-disaster look: shirt sleeves neatly rolled up, hands on hips, brand-new hiking boots.

Politicians can go overboard on the disaster damage tour: over-promising help, exaggerating their empathy, and all the while angling to be on TV. Clinton did none of that. Instead, she used humor, and it worked perfectly.

During their tour, the Clinton group entered a home destroyed by the flood. Water had turned everything over, busted through walls, and left the flooring covered in mud and sewage.

As twenty politicians and reporters crowded into the living room, they ran smack dab into the woman who had lived there. She seemed exhausted and surprised by the visit.

Disaster survivor encounters in front of the media can be dicey. You never know how homeowners will react. They may be angry. They're certainly dealing with heavy emotions. No one on this tour could provide federal help because the President hadn't yet declared the flood a major disaster.

The politicians grew quiet, not knowing what to say to the homeowner. It was a high-profile tour, a signature moment in front of the media to show local, state, and national leader engagement. Everyone tensed up except Clinton, who charged right up to the homeowner. She looked around the room in awe and said, "Wow! What the heck happened here?"

At once, the woman relaxed her shoulders and smiled. "It was a big flood," she said.

Clinton leaned in and stroked her arm. "Yes, it was," she said. "Yes, it was."

I struggled with talking to disaster survivors early in my career for a long time. The encounters always felt awkward. I tried too hard to prove empathy. I thought I had an obligation to solve all their problems immediately.

Then I realized the best way to connect is by just being curious. Whenever I met survivors, I asked tons of questions. I wanted to hear their story. I wanted to know what the heck happened. I'd ask them to tell me about the damage, how their family was doing, and whether they had applied for disaster help. I wanted to know what they were doing now, who had helped them, and who they had helped. I'd repeat things they told me throughout the conversation to let them know I was listening. I told them when I felt they'd taken the proper steps toward their recovery.

Interviewing them is about more than providing comfort. It also helps you gather information, which you can then use to help the community.

STUDY HISTORY

Twenty years after the 9/11 terrorist attacks, Rudy Giuliani became a distracting character in American politics. His complicated legacy is a shame from an emergency management perspective because we forget we can learn a lot from how he handled the immediate aftermath. Following Hurricane Katrina—four years later and while he was still widely respected—Louisianians would tell us, "I wish Giuliani were our mayor."

If you look at news clips from 2001, Giuliani might strike you as a taller man. What made him appear prominent was not his height but his stride. He never appeared in public as hesitant. He walked with purpose, whether through the city's makeshift EOC at Pier 92 or leading a tour at Ground Zero. This observation may seem like a small thing, but after 9/11, the nation's leadership needed to show they weren't cowering. And at the time, Giuliani was one of the most-watched people in the world.

During the post-9/11 news conferences, which Giuliani initially held twice daily, he stood at the podium surrounded by an army of responders. It included functional components of the response—fire, police, emergency management, medical—and local, state, and federal leaders. Everyone wore a uniform, or at least their agency's hat. The image conveyed a powerful, one team, one response, "we got this" message that was essential after 9/11.

When you work in disasters, it helps to become a disaster history nerd. You'll never know where you might find an old trick to solve a modern problem. Giuliani later recalled that the night before the attacks, he had been reading a biography of Winston Churchill. When Giuliani addressed the impact of 9/11, he discussed how the city would come back from the event. He used a classic Churchill technique: confront the challenge and express optimism for overcoming it.

Studying history may also offer more concrete solutions. I asked a London fire chief how the city's fire brigade initially communicated between command posts during the "7/7" bombings on July 7, 2005.

"Cell phones? Radios?" I asked.

"No," he said. "Couldn't count on modern technology."

"What then?"

"Something we've kept in our toolbox but haven't used for generations: human runners."

It's a simple solution, but not one that immediately comes to mind during a catastrophe.

BECOME A CRISIS OPTIMIST

When asked in a TV interview what helped him get through the early days after 9/11, Giuliani said, "I'm an optimist." The media often tells responders, survivors, and the public that they face insurmountable disaster challenges—the end of the world as we know it. It seems every reporter lives for the moment when they can dramatically say, "The world has changed forever."

An American responder I talked with had a different take. "Has there ever been a devastating crisis our country has not eventually overcome? I can't think of one. Why not be a crisis optimist? It is nothing more than believing in the resiliency of people."

The explorer Ernest Shackleton was another crisis leader who self-identified as an optimist. Shackleton led a 1914 expedition to Antarctica, and Caroline Alexander captured his story rivetingly in *The Endurance: Shackleton's Legendary Antarctic Expedition.*

While approaching Antarctica, the expedition's ship, *Endurance,* got stuck in the ice floes, slowly got crushed, and, after fifteen months, sank. After abandoning the sinking vessel, Shackleton and his twenty-seven-member crew, surviving off seal meat and penguins, traveled to Elephant Island.

Once his shipmates had established rudimentary shelter on the island, Shackleton embarked on a 22.5-foot open boat with five crew members to find help. They set out for South Georgia Island. After an eight-hundred-mile, two-week journey across the Southern Ocean, they landed on the island's southern shore. Shackleton then hiked over the island's mountains to reach a whaling station on the north coast and organized a rescue effort. After repeated tries, Shackleton returned to his remaining twenty-two crew on Elephant Island and brought them all back to safety, twenty-four months and twenty-two days after the expedition had set sail from England.

Shackleton had an ambitious dream. He wanted to be the first person to cross Antarctica. This dream ended in dramatic failure. And how did he describe his favorite quality in a person?

"Optimism," he said. "Especially optimism in the face of reverses and apparent defeat."

Shackleton was successful because he changed his mission goal. Shackleton adjusted once it became plain that they were in dire trouble, as any good crisis leader would. Thanks to his optimism, the new plan became not to traverse the continent but to survive and make sure all those with him did as well—which they did.

CRISIS OPTIMISTS CHANGE THEIR LANGUAGE

How do you refer to the people affected by disaster? The ones looking for help, guidance, and information to begin their recovery? You might think of them as either victims or survivors. The word you choose matters.

There is implicit power in calling people "survivors." It signals strength and control, while "victim" implies helplessness and an uncertain future. That does not mean sugarcoating real problems these survivors face.

Have bad things occurred? Sure.

Will it be hard? Yes.

Will things be the same as before? Doubtful.

Yet buildings can be rebuilt and people helped, allowing communities to bounce back. Being a crisis optimist does not mean ignoring the real challenges of recovering from a disaster. It's the belief that you can help people overcome them, survive, and rebuild. And it's a belief that people have the power to be part of that recovery process.

The language of a crisis optimist has three parts:

1. It's from the heart. The words of crisis optimists inspire because they are real and not spoken from cue cards.
2. It includes positive self-talk. You call yourself an optimist.
3. It's not fake or over the top. You will lose credibility with your team and disaster survivors, who can spot phony optimism from a mile away.

Now that we've looked at ways to step up, let's examine what you should avoid doing. Who doesn't step up? Deflators, pilers-on, and delusional optimists. Let's examine each one:

DEFLATORS

One evening a few years into my emergency management career, I shared an elevator ride to the lobby with FEMA director Wallace Stickney and several high-ranking officials from the "8th Floor"—where all critical decisions get made.

The officials surrounding Stickney seemed exhausted and kept letting out deep sighs. One said, "Well, at least another day, another dollar." They acted so put-upon with burdens.

They kept looking at Stickney and expecting commiseration. He stoically stared at them. I got the sense that he was embarrassed by their talk. Later, Stickney put out a message to employees quoting President Theodore Roosevelt's 1910 "Man in the Arena" speech. In the speech, Roosevelt says:

> It's not the critic who counts, nor the man who points out how the strong man stumbles, or where the doer of deeds could have done them better. The credit belongs to the man who is actually in the arena, whose face is marred by dust and sweat and blood;

who errs, who comes up short again and again because there is no effort without error and shortcoming; but who does actually strive to do the deeds, who knows great enthusiasm, the great devotions; who spends himself in a worthy cause; who at best knows the triumph of high achievement, and who at the worst, if he fails, at least fails while daring greatly, so that his place shall never be with those cold and timid souls who neither know victory or defeat.

I always wondered if he did that in part based on the elevator scene that evening, and that's what he wished he had said then. Whenever I think of Stickney, I always connect these two events for some reason. It's what I remember most about him and his tenure as FEMA director.

The whole scene in the elevator bothered me then, and I've never forgotten it. My takeaway: don't become the type of emergency manager who shows you're ready to give up. Instead, appreciate the privilege of being a person in the arena. I made a mental note. If I ever got a leadership position in emergency management and found myself forgetting this, it was time to quit.

PILERS-ON

Watch out for those who "pile on" to disasters, who want to make disasters seem more than they are. They reject any accomplishment, pointing out only what remains incomplete.

These hyper-negative people fabricate new negative scenarios about how a disaster will worsen. They become enraptured by visions of the next wave of devastation and tend to exaggerate the current one. There's even a scientific term for this: it's called catastrophizing. Here's an example. Months after one disaster hit, a community advocate continued to tell Congress and the media that displaced flood survivors had no safe place to live. His rhetorical calls for help kept spreading. In one tear-filled and widely televised plea, he described survivors living in cars, tents, and on the streets.

A disaster housing officer met with him. "Look," she said. "It's my responsibility to help people find a safe place to live while they start rebuilding their homes. I'm not seeing the problems you're seeing. But if they're out there, I have emergency housing options available right now. I can help the people you keep talking about. Help me get in touch with them."

The advocate couldn't identify a single name or provide a specific example. He was reliving the early days after the disaster and was blinded to the recovery progress taking place in his community.

DELUSIONAL OPTIMISTS

In the 2009 movie *The Informant!*, a whistleblower exposing price-fixing and bribery at Archer Midland Daniels huddles with the FBI for the big raid at the firm to capture incriminating evidence.

"Now, when this goes down," he's told, "everything is going to change for you."

Impressively naïve about the situation, the informant, played by Matt Damon, asks his FBI handlers, "You think I'll still be okay at the company, though, right?"

Everyone stares at him. "Well," says the District Attorney, "I think the corporate culture might change a little bit for you…"

Damon's character remains undaunted. His dreams of grandeur include the belief that his takedown of the company will pole-vault him to position as CEO by a grateful board of directors, and he nods enthusiastically. "Well, I should hope so!"

Delusional optimists have unrealistic expectations about surmounting obstacles and overestimate their capacity to affect change. Sometimes their insane enthusiasm can be contagious. You have to dial them down before others get caught in their web.

I need to stress something here. I'm not suggesting *not* going for it. By all means, reach for the stars. Put a man on the moon. But don't try to convince people you're putting a man on the moon without a rocket ship. Make sure your ambitions—and your promises—are based on some sort of capabilities and reason, and you're acknowledging challenges and doing something about them.

We hope for the best and plan for the worst in the disaster world. The delusional optimist prepares for the best and never considers anything else—the proverbial burying your head in the sand.

BE A POSITIVE FORCE OF NATURE

I just laid out for you examples of how (and how not) to step up. You can try these tips and see if they're right for you. There's no definite list of how you contribute during a disaster. But I've seen them work.

At the beginning of the chapter, I mentioned the Chinese proverb of Yin and Yang. You'll find it's a popular philosophical
metaphor for emergency management. Crisis leaders train
disaster workers to see opportunities during a crisis. I've seen
responders hang posters of the symbol in their offices.

For instance, there's even a silver lining to delusional optimists.
They create an opportunity for someone brave enough to step
into the void and make their mark.

Once, FEMA needed someone to step up and run its community relations program during a widespread storm. After an
incident, federal-state community relations teams connect with
local officials. They visit impacted neighborhoods to identify
unmet needs and provide survivors with recovery information.

During this particular disaster, the mission took a while to get
going. Some in the agency—delusional optimists—had overestimated the program's readiness capability. The agency struggled
to deploy staff from around the country to the disaster scene.
Frustrated leaders of the response pounded the desk. They
looked for someone to take responsibility for leading community relations, fixing the deployment delay, and getting the staff
into the field. Not many people working the disaster raised their
hands and said "pick me."

Finally, they turned to a young woman who had just arrived
from Kansas City. Her name was Merideth Parrish. Senior
response officials didn't know much about Merideth. She hadn't
been with the agency long. But they asked if she'd be willing to
step up and take charge.

"Okay," Merideth said. "Got it."

She then rose to the occasion like a "positive force of nature—full of energy, unstoppable, and unforgettable." (Credit for this phrase belongs to Anna Pridmore, a civil infrastructure rehabilitation advisor, who used it in an unrelated article).

Merideth would oversee one of the most extensive community relations operations in the agency's history, managing more than a thousand people. Under her leadership, the outreach teams identified emergency requirements, supported local response organizations, and helped tens of thousands of families start their recovery. It was Merideth's most prominent disaster assignment in her career with the agency and her FEMA legacy moment.

People who step up and seize opportunities have a can-do attitude. They're willing to take on disaster assignments when asked, even if they feel they may not be ready enough. I think most crisis leaders are fine with this. They'd rather have a daring "I got it" instead of a roomful of people saying "I don't want it."

I remember a remarkable thing when Merideth got her chance to step up. She didn't hesitate. She seemed as if she had been waiting for such an opportunity. And like many people who enter emergency management for all the right reasons, when such an opportunity arose, she seemed determined to step up with enthusiasm and positive energy. She seemed determined to make a difference. And that's precisely what she did.

CHAPTER 3

Think in Threes

ONE WAY TO CONQUER CRISIS CHAOS

"I have just three things to teach: simplicity, patience, compassion. These three are your greatest treasures."

—LAO TZU

An incident responder briefs the media on operational priorities during the Waldo Canyon Fire in 2012. *Photo by Michael Rieger/FEMA*

I have interviewed with thousands of reporters and conducted countless briefings for communities, government officials, Congressional members, and their staff. Yet I've always struggled with public speaking. I'm fine working off memorized talking points or a scripted presentation. But I often melt down during impromptu situations, like a question-and-answer session or an unexpected encounter in the hall with someone I admire. I've even stumbled while explaining what I did in disaster situations to neighbors and friends in social settings.

I'm terrible at explaining operational concepts. My thoughts seem clear in my mind, but when they come out of my mouth, they're bafflegab.

This condition held me back early on in my emergency management career. I often had good ideas but didn't speak up because I wasn't confident about sharing my thoughts aloud. When I did go for it, I would have the agonizing realization that my answers or explanations fell short. I confused my listeners instead of impressing them. I let these fumbles bother me for a long time.

Then I realized my issue was an organizational one. I stumbled on a common management technique that helped me become a better communicator. I went from being scared to speak at high-profile meetings to publicly representing the federal government during high-profile disasters. It's called: "Thinking in Threes."

What are three things you remember the CDC asking you to do as COVID-19 cases surged early in the pandemic? Three stick out in my mind:

1. Wash your hands.
2. Keep six feet of distance.
3. Wear a mask.

The CDC focused its public health guidance on these *three* straightforward and actionable instructions because they were simple, effective, and easy to remember.

In this chapter, we're going to break down the process of thinking in threes, why it's valuable, and how to do it.

THE VALUE OF THINKING IN THREES

Former baseball manager Tommy Lasorda also recognized the value of threes when he said, "There are three types of baseball players: those who make it happen, those who watch it happen, and those who wonder what happened."

There's a reason we call three the perfect number. Let's put on your responder cap for a moment. You're navigating new experiences, finding unexpected challenges, and juggling multiple issues every day. To avoid being overwhelmed, psychologists recommend cutting the pie into smaller pieces. Making things more minor and less formidable can have a calming effect and remove action paralysis. Many refer to this technique as the emergency management definition of the divide-and-conquer theory.

Making things manageable makes "thinking in threes" a power-house tool for disaster responders and emergency management, bringing order to an otherwise chaotic environment.

THINKING IN THREES CAN HELP YOU CONQUER CRISIS CHAOS

When a disaster first happens, there is a deficit of information. No one knows how widespread the event is or how the incident impacted people. We call this "the information void" time. Soon, government officials, legacy and social media, community leaders, and survivors fill that void with official and unofficial announcements. It quickly evolves from everyone searching for answers to getting bombarded with news. Now you've gone from information void to information overload.

These phases—not enough information and too much information—can cause chaos and confusion. Your mind can go wacky trying to get a handle on it. Here's how one response team explained using the "thinking in threes" principle to manage the information challenge.

"We constantly broke the disaster down into our top three issues. Then we figured out the first three things we needed to do for each issue. What looked complicated became less so once we developed that plan. Did we make some educated guesses? Of course. Did we miss some pieces at the beginning? No doubt. But if we hadn't started, we would have missed everything."

THINKING IN THREES CAN HELP YOU KICK-START YOUR PRIORITIES

When our FEMA public affairs team from Denver landed in New York after 9/11, the first three things we decided to do were:

1. Find a hotel for the next few nights.

2. Get to the Javits Center and connect with the national search team leadership.
3. Reach out to our counterparts in the city.

Were these the best three things we could have done first? It didn't matter. What mattered was that we did *something*.

The hardest priorities to establish when working in a disaster are the first ones. Resources you counted on may not be available. There might not be power, for example. Communications may be limited. The chain of command and organizational structure may not be apparent or fully formed. Regardless of your position, it's highly unlikely anyone else has much time to think for you. You will need to think for yourself.

Disasters will tempt you to try doing everything at once. You need to prioritize what to do first. Don't worry about being perfect. Choose any three things to do. Almost without fail, you'll be in the ballpark. If not, you can constantly adjust. The idea is just to get moving—and create early momentum. The priority-setting will be natural once you get into the response groove.

Jim Chesnutt, who worked in public affairs for FEMA, liked to say, "I like three. In the early phase of the disaster, who can accomplish more than that?"

Once, a well-intentioned colleague gave me feedback on my job performance in the early days during a disaster assignment. Though unsolicited, I welcomed the insights. Yet after our hour-long meeting, I ended up with pages full of his suggestions—and still no clear sense of what I should do in the next twenty-four hours, which is what I really needed to know.

Giving someone like me ten, fifteen, or twenty things to do at that stage of the disaster was a waste of time and effort. The situation would change before I got very far. I spent more time analyzing the list he gave me than acting on it.

THINKING IN THREES HELPS YOU FOLLOW THE PATTERNS

Disasters unfold in layers, and often this occurs in a pattern of three. It's bizarre, but it happens all the time.

In 2011, Japan experienced three nearly simultaneous disasters. In March of that year, a magnitude 9.0 earthquake triggered a tsunami, which then caused a meltdown at the Fukushima Daiichi Nuclear Power Plant.

During the 9/11 attacks, the Wahhabi Islamic terrorist group Al-Qaeda had three targets: the World Trade Center, the Pentagon, and the US Capitol or the White House.

Hurricane Katrina unfolded in a series of cascading events: first the hurricane, which led to levee failure, and then a massive flood.

Thinking in threes reminds you to, as FEMA's Bob Fenton once said, "Keep one eye on what I got now, and one eye on what is looming out there."

By the way, Bob said this in Louisiana in 2008—during the aftermath of Katrina, when responding to Hurricane Gustav, and while preparing for Hurricane Ike. See the pattern of threes?

LEADERS USE THE POWER OF THREES ALL THE TIME

Leaders naturally gravitate to "thinking in threes" because it's effective. Jeff Bezos, founder of the e-commerce company Amazon, is one example. He says, "We've had three big ideas at Amazon that we've stuck with for eighteen years, and they're the reason we're successful: Put the customer first. Invent. And be patient."

Messaging by local officials during the initial COVID-19 response in 2020 provides another example. The emergence of the pandemic was the epitome of a chaotic, confusing, and rapidly developing crisis situation that required a tool for organizing thoughts and communicating priorities. If you look back at the early months of the world's response to the pandemic, I'm sure you can identify a crisis leader you thought rose to the occasion. Whoever you picked, I'm guessing that they did three things well:

They described the crisis in a concrete way anybody could understand. They explained:

- what the coronavirus was (a disease);
- what it looked like (the symptoms); and
- how it was transmitted (close person-to-person contact).

By sharing this information, leaders helped make COVID-19 less scary and more understandable.

They had a plan with specific actions. For example, it might have included:

- issuing isolation guidance to reduce transmission;
- obtaining medical supplies to care for critically ill patients; and
- providing financial assistance to those impacted.

They told the public things they could do to get help, help others, and stay informed, such as:

- applying for unemployment assistance;
- assisting vulnerable family members; and
- checking for updates on official websites.

Naturally, or purposefully, exceptional crisis leaders have a knack for using the power of threes to tackle emergencies. You don't need to be an elected official to adopt this principle. Anyone can do it. All it takes is recognizing how thinking in threes might help you manage your responsibilities.

REMEMBER, IT'S A TOOL, NOT A RULE

Thinking in threes should not limit your ability to do your job. Consider this principle not as a strict rule but as a tool to manage your priorities. You're not going to do everything in groups of three. That would be excessive. Use this organizational tool when it makes sense to use it.

For instance, it might help you:

- identify issues;
- explain operational activities; and
- establish goals for your team.

Let's look at examples of each of these.

IDENTIFYING ISSUES

The Columbine High School massacre happened twelve miles from my office when I worked at the Denver Federal Center. Eric Harris and Dylan Klebold showed up at their school on April 20, 1999, and started killing their classmates. We had employees with children who went to that school, so this tragedy was deeply personal.

When the shooting stopped, Jim Chesnutt and I headed to the Jefferson County incident command post in the public library at Columbine Park, adjacent to the high school. There we connected with Steve Davis from the sheriff's department, who ran the daily press conference updates for the hundreds of reporters who had arrived at the scene. We became his support team, doing whatever he needed, including monitoring the news coverage to clarify or correct reporting after his briefings.

My assignment at Columbine sparked a lifelong interest in school safety. Whenever I heard of a disaster, one of my first thoughts was, "What is the impact on the schools?"

Not many institutions are more symbolic of a community's vulnerability—or its resilience—than its schools. And few accomplishments signify disaster recovery more than whether the schools have been repaired, rebuilt, and reopened.

Despite my interest in the subject, I struggled to find common lessons from school incidents that I could share with local emergency managers. There did not seem to be much connection between a Columbine incident and, say, a tornado on the Pine Ridge Indian Reservation in South Dakota.

Then one day, I met the principal of East High School in Denver, Colorado. She talked about her experience from a recent fire and mentioned she had studied other school emergencies. I asked for her help. "Tell me the top issues you see when it comes to schools and disasters."

She told me there are three things that stand out to her, regardless of the cause of the disaster:

1. **Schools must have their emergency plan within arm's reach.** "Even if it sits in your desk drawer and you don't pull it out until something happens. It gives you something to hold on to and refer to, and the guidance needed to make quick decisions."
2. **Schools need to build a comprehensive network of contacts.** "We tend to be too insular, thinking only of academic responsibilities. We need to do a better job of building relationships outside our education network. When the disaster hits, you need to know who your buddy is at emergency management, and at the police department, the fire station, at the Red Cross, for health information, or even at the weather service."
3. **Schools need to have a more robust capability for accessing and providing crisis counseling.** "After a disaster, you'll need this service more than you think and for longer than you'd expected."

I put these principal observations to the test. I bounced them off a teacher at the Pine Ridge Indian Reservation elementary school whose young students rushed to the window every time the sky grew dark, in fear of a tornado. I shared them with a school superintendent who rebuilt school after school following a series of catastrophic floods. And I asked for feedback from my friend Kate Stetzner, a former principal who later became an educational leadership advisor for the US Department of Homeland Security and for school districts.

In 1994, as the principal at Margaret Leary Elementry School in Butte, Montana, Kate helped her community navigate the aftermath of a schoolyard murder involving—at the time—the youngest school shooter in American history. While Kate's students lined up for assembly, a ten-year-old boy pulled out a .22 semiautomatic handgun and opened fire, killing eleven-year-old classmate Jeremy Bullock.

Kate and all the others agreed with these three lessons on school safety and recovery. One school superintendent told me he became a regular participant on conference calls with the National Weather Service, "which gave us a direct heads-up on any storm event that might impact our students."

When I was dealing with a pile of issues, I would make a goal to identify the top three. As an emergency manager, your job involves paying attention to what's happening in disaster land. You're a problem finder, issue gatherer, and feedback collector, but you can't have a thousand yellow-sticky-note action items and expect to be efficient. You need to organize those sticky notes into categories like the principal from Denver did.

EXPLAINING OPERATIONAL ACTIVITIES

One of the best ways to appreciate this principle is by observing it in action during disaster news conferences. Pay attention to an incident commander at the scene of a storm, fire, or flood. During a wildland fire briefing, for instance, three priorities I often hear are:

1. firefighter safety
2. protecting homes and infrastructure
3. managing the fire (by putting it out, containing it, or letting it burn)

When you start watching for the principle, you'll be surprised how often incident responders use it to explain a situation or outline priorities. Here are some more examples.

What are the recovery priorities?
- housing assistance
- infrastructure repair
- mitigation measures

What was the disaster like? I remember:
- daily briefings to keep people informed,
- the flooding caused more damage than the hurricane winds, and
- storm debris stacked six feet high on every block.

What was the purpose of FEMA's 9/11 photo/video mission?

- Document the event for history,
- share images with the news media, and
- help train future urban search and rescue teams.

How are you evaluating the housing need? I'm:

- reading damage reports,
- talking to residents, and
- doing a drive-by to eyeball it myself.

What's a standard training tool to prepare crisis spokespersons for media interviews?

- What happened?
- What are you doing about it?
- What does it mean to me?

Why didn't you bring a hardhat?

- Training told me I didn't need one.
- I thought someone would have an extra one.
- I didn't know earthquakes had aftershocks.

I made the last one up, but I hope you agree that the rest make sense, come across clearly, and are action-oriented.

In 2003, as the East Coast geared up for Hurricane Isabel, the Governor of Virginia, Mark Warner, asked FEMA's David Fuku-tomi to say a few words during a media briefing at the state emergency operations center.

Fukutomi held up one, two, and three fingers at the podium while he spoke. "FEMA has three forms of assistance you need to be aware of right now," he said.

"One, direct federal assistance for emergency needs in the community, which means we can provide the state food, water, or resources like search and rescue teams.

"Two, individual assistance for people means grants for families to help them get back on their feet and begin their recovery.

"Three, public infrastructure assistance. These are grants to help you replace, repair, rebuild, and restore your public facilities damaged by the storm—things like fire stations, roads, schools—and also to reimburse local governments for expenses they incur for items like shelters and evacuations."

Unlike with David's succinct summary, I am surprised how often people struggle to explain what they do in a concise way. Some people tie themselves into verbal knots when explaining what their organization does when disaster strikes. I struggled with this early in my career, too. One of the best ways to practice communicating in threes is to describe your emergency management job in three brief points. Don't just think about them in your head. Say them out loud to make sure they make sense.

While looking for threes, judge whether the priorities make sense to you or how you might improve them. When you hear phrasing that resonates, save it to use yourself later.

ESTABLISHING TEAM GOALS

You can also use thinking in threes when communicating with your team. Perhaps you're kicking off a new initiative or need to shift momentum or focus. But you can't waste chances to explain your goals. You have to be ready when you have everyone's attention.

Sometimes crisis leaders miss opportunities to communicate their goals, or don't do it well. Myself included.

Working in the Western Pacific after a typhoon, I sent one of our video shooters to Chuuk Island and other parts of the Federated States of Micronesia. The videographer I sent was the first vegan I had ever met. He loved animals. Once at dinner, he sent his plate of rice back three times because he was sure some animal parts had fallen into it.

Before he left for Chuuk, I told him to get lots of video documentation of survivors, not only the damages. I assumed he understood I wanted shots of 1) individuals, 2) families, and 3) island leaders.

When he returned home, I asked our documentation producer if the footage included survivors recovering from the typhoon.

"Technically, yes," she said.

"What do you mean *technically*?" I asked.

"Damn, if he didn't get a video of every dog, cat, and pig he saw."

GREAT MESSAGE, WRONG AUDIENCE

I once worked with a high-ranking federal executive who would hold "all hands" meetings and spend the entire hour talking about recycling. During the meetings, a room packed with disaster responders saw visuals on what was not recyclable. They received a demonstration on the proper disposal of reusable trash—the blue bins—and a lecture on why this was important with lots of impressive data.

During the recycling leader's tenure, I asked a few people in the office what our top three priorities were. More than once, someone said, "… Uh… Recycling, and, um, other stuff." I think they were joking.

I am pro-recycling and have retained quite a bit from these mandatory meetings, which changed my behavior for the better. Yet "all hands" meetings are precious. It is a rare opportunity to emphasize the organization's mission and connect everyone to that mission.

GREAT MESSAGE, RIGHT AUDIENCE

On the other hand, I have seen crisis leaders employ the "thinking in threes" technique to establish team goals and they've done it well. Here are some I remember from my FEMA days.

When Gary Briese worked at FEMA, he made preparing for no-notice events such as earthquakes one of his top priorities. Jerry DeFelice recalled Briese roaming the office hallways to check in on his staff. "He asked me three questions," said DeFelice: 'tell me what you're doing, tell me why you're doing it, and tell me how it relates to earthquakes.'"

Some leaders also employ the threes principle to share their motto. When he ran disasters for FEMA, Mike Byrne used to post his motto on large signs in the hallways. "Commitment, Compassion, Courage," the sign said. I don't know if anyone told Mike this, but his staff liked those words, and quoted them to each other quite a bit.

After James Lee Witt became FEMA director in 1993, he described the agency as "people helping people." FEMA put this axiom on the back of its field shirts. Decades later—as I conducted research for this book—several long-time responders spontaneously used this three-word catchphrase when I asked them to explain the disaster relief mission.

As a regional administrator, Rick Weiland wanted to build emergency management capabilities in Indian Country, particularly in the upper Midwest plains and the intermountain areas of Utah, Wyoming, and Colorado, home to twenty-nine Tribal Nations.

He defined his goal this way: "I want to know what FEMA can do for the tribes. I want to know what an emergency management program can do for the tribes. And I want to know what the tribes can teach us about emergency preparedness and disaster response. It's an opportunity for us. It's a legal obligation for us. And, it's time."

In 2009, Tony Russell took over the federal Louisiana recovery office for Hurricanes Katrina, Rita, Gustav, and Ike. He wanted to repair intergovernmental relationships, break the logjam of delayed infrastructure assistance grants, and help shift the recovery momentum.

He said the same three things at every staff meeting, community gathering, and media appearance.

"First, we're going to take a fresh look at every eligibility decision. Second, everything we do from now on will be in cooperation with—and will need the cooperation of—everyone who has a stake in the outcome. Third, together, as one federal-state-local team, our goal is to cut red tape, rebuild hurricane-damaged public facilities, and restore essential government services."

As you can see, there are many different ways leaders make use of this principle. While some emergency management professionals waste leadership message moments, others use their influence in concert with memorable phrasing to emphasize preparing for earthquakes, prioritizing customer service, building emergency management capabilities in Indian Country, or reenergizing recovery programs.

When you have an audience primed and ready for inspiration from you, their leader, give them your best three thoughts, not three whiffs—as in a strikeout.

IN DEDICATION...

In 2003, I spoke at an emergency management conference in Lake Traverse, Michigan. I shared the stage with Captain Alfred "Al" Clair Haynes, hero of United Airlines Flight 232. En route to Chicago from Denver with 285 passengers and eleven crew members aboard on July 19, 1989, Flight 232's tail engine blew up. Haynes lost the ability to operate the plane's hydraulics.

Haynes steered the plane to a crash landing in Sioux City, Iowa, using the thruster controls of his two remaining engines to keep the wings level. While Flight 232 wobbled in, Woodbury County emergency services director Gary Brown, who had participated in a multi-agency plane crash exercise two years earlier, mobilized all his resources and waited at the airport.

During the approach, Haynes could not reduce the plane's speed. He needed to maintain power thrusts to keep from tilting and spiraling out of control. Flight 232 came in hard and fast and broke into three pieces, killing 112 people on the plane.

Unbelievably, however, 184 people survived. The National Transportation Safety Board credited Haynes and the flight crew for their ability to stay calm and land the plane, and Brown for having his community crisis-ready.

Following our presentations, Haynes and I shared a sandwich at the cafeteria. We talked about the 1992 TV movie about the accident (*Crash Landing: The Rescue of Flight 232*), with Haynes portrayed by Charlton Heston. I'm not sure whether he liked the movie. However, he did tell me he liked the three themes of the dedication at the film's end:

Dedicated to those who died, those who survived, and those who prepared.

CHAPTER 4

Own It

HOW TO BUILD INTERAGENCY TEAMS

"Action springs not from thought, but from a readiness for responsibility."

—DIETRICH BONHOEFFER

The American Red Cross delivers meals in a Long Island neighborhood as survivors return home to begin cleanup and repair work following widespread flooding during Superstorm Sandy. Photo by Andrea Booher/FEMA.

Post-Katrina, FEMA helped tens of thousands of families relocate to mobile homes and camper-style travel trailers while waiting for more permanent housing. Then, community leaders discovered that some units contained a high level of formaldehyde. Some people in the government argued the levels presented health risks, especially to young children and those with breathing problems, and that there was no remedy except to move out. Others insisted the levels weren't more than those prevalent in a new car and could be reduced to safe levels with ventilation by simply opening windows and doors.

Despite mounting evidence of widespread community concern about formaldehyde in specific units, some government officials remained convinced that relatively few people had raised serious health risks. Others cited a lack of testing standards. Field staff for the housing operation sought legal advice about more testing. They were reportedly told to avoid involvement because that "would imply FEMA ownership of the [legal] issue," according to congressional testimony. But worries emanating from the local level didn't disappear. They grew from a few complaints to hundreds, congressional involvement, and a class-action lawsuit against several manufacturers, which was later settled.

In a crisis, even the perception of a health concern must be treated as a legitimate one. Indeed, after conducting tests, the Centers for Disease Control and Prevention (CDC) confirmed in a February 14, 2008 report that "at the levels seen in many trailers, health could be affected" and cautioned against long-term exposure during warmer weather. ("Evaluation of Formaldehyde Levels in Occupied Federal Emergency Management Agency-Owned Temporary Housing Units," 2007.)

FEMA administrator Dave Paulison eventually took charge of the issue. Paulison traveled to the Gulf Coast. He shared the CDC results publicly, ordered more testing, and apologized. The agency began moving survivors with health concerns to hotels, motels, and apartments until better, longer-term accommodations could be found. (As of 2022, FEMA still uses mobile homes and recreational-type campers for temporary and emergency housing in coordination with health authorities and state and local officials. The units now have higher safety and manufacturer standards, and the issues from Hurricane Katrina have been resolved, according to agency statements.)

WEIGHING THE CONSEQUENCES OF OWNING DISASTER PROBLEMS

Everyone in emergency management will eventually face a situation when a problem emerges and somebody needs to step up and own it. Taking responsibility can be scary. It means holding yourself accountable in front of your peers, organizational leadership, political leadership, the media, and the public. Disaster history provides plenty of examples where crisis leaders accepted responsibility, and people still criticized them.

Owning issues during a crisis and sticking with that decision is challenging for any leader. Recovery from a disaster is difficult. It takes time. It takes enormous energy. It takes resources. Those who step up can become a target for frustration and blame.

Despite the best efforts of any capable crisis leader, there will be recovery winners and losers. Some people won't bounce back as well as others. The assistance will never arrive as fast as you want. Good people on your team will quit their jobs or retire early. Energy fades. People grow tired. And disaster fatigue can cause even the most dedicated leaders to lose perspective during the endless parade of major decisions. At the local level, mayors lose elections.

Yet when emergency managers—and, by extension, local leaders—own up, inevitably their intergovernmental and interagency teammates benefit, which means disaster survivors do, too. This principle is not for the faint of heart. Owning responsibility comes with consequences. You may receive unfair criticism, harm your reputation, or damage your career. But in emergency management you are given the gift of responsibility. You have no choice but to use that to make a difference.

My sense is we're destined for a new era of leadership and expectations for leaders. Many people believe the current generation of political leadership has perfected the art of deferment. They want all the credit, none of the blame, and zero accountability. Everything is always someone else's fault. I gather that the emerging generation is fed up and not afraid to call it out. Expect the next generation of crisis leaders to be held to higher standards.

The reassuring news is that you'll find good crisis leaders who already accept responsibility routinely with confidence and commitment. Exceptional leaders do it with joy and excitement, which may sound strange to non-emergency workers. But there's nothing wrong with people being happy about the chance to fix something and help someone. The very best do all the above and act like the crisis was made for them—and they were made for it.

The three choices leaders have during a crisis:

1. Blame someone else for the problem.
2. Hide from the situation.
3. Own the problem.

Let's take a deeper look at these choices.

BLAME SOMEONE ELSE FOR THE PROBLEM

A self-described "policy wonk," former Louisiana Governor Bobby Jindal was one smart dude. He quickly climbed the professional ranks and had tremendous career success at a young age. In 2004, he ran for Congress and won. In 2007, at age thirty-six, Louisianans elected him governor of the state. In 2010, he published a book, *Leadership and Crisis*.

I worked as an External Affairs Officer for FEMA during the Louisiana response to Hurricane Gustav in 2008, and Jindal ran one of the best Incident Command meetings of any disaster I've seen. The governor had a clear set of priorities, usually between three and five, for every meeting, including repatriation of evacuees, debris removal, commodity distribution, power restoration, and recovery centers.

The governor moved item by item down his list of issues, asking questions to understand any obstacles standing in the way. Favoring quantitative analysis, he demanded facts, numbers, deadlines, and statistics to define problems and measure accomplishments. He scribbled everything down on a notepad as fast as possible throughout the meeting.

Jindal recognized that the hurricane response required many government agencies and private sector resources. Any organization that could supply help or technical skill received an invitation to attend his early evening command meetings. He tossed out encouraging remarks to attendees.

"We love you, Mike, but we need to do better," Jindal told Mike Hall, the federal coordinating officer for the disaster.

By the end of these hour-long sessions, Jindal would have a plan and a team inspired to work together. Then he would dash out of the meeting into a press conference and blast the federal government for its response.

It wasn't just a jab or tempered remark shaded with praise and a sprinkle of thanks for what was working. No, the most powerful man in the state would deliver a flat-out sucker punch to the gut. And he would go on and on. Playing the governor's remarks back years later, it came across like this in my mind:

> Here's your tough governor, fighting for you during every step of your recovery, and let me tell you, the federal government is so screwed up. They are making our job hard. But we're going to fix everything. Everything good happening right now is thanks to our state agencies, and you, the survivors. Everything you don't like is out of our control because it belongs to the federal government.

As I saw it, minutes after building up a response team privately, Jindal would blast one of his teammates publicly. Interagency communication, coordination, and a sense of cooperation would take a hit. Ultimately, I thought it was counterproductive to the mission. It became a sideshow we had to deal with, fogging our view of the path to resolve disaster-related issues.

Of all the issues to emerge after Gustav, commodity distribution raised Jindal's ire the most. When FEMA provides food, water, and life-sustaining supplies for a disaster, actual delivery to survivors is a shared responsibility of federal, state, and local agencies.

FEMA brings relief goods into the state. State and local agencies set up distribution centers to manage and pass out the supplies to survivors. As with every form of assistance in a disaster, agencies must coordinate to get commodities to people who need them.

Hurricane Gustav had caused damage across a wide area, destroying more than ten thousand homes. Debris-clogged roads slowed delivery trucks and power crews working to restore electricity, so they rarely reached distribution points when expected.

Another contributing factor was how the National Guard handed out supplies at the distribution centers. No one questioned the need, but the daily volume of commodities going out the door exceeded FEMA's metrics based on the number of people affected. Commodities flew out the door, and distribution centers ran out of food while people waited in line.

As the volume of supplies bled out, FEMA depleted its immediate stockpile and reached deep into the Department of Defense reserve supply. "Refill the pipeline, keep the distribution channels open, and run the trucks twenty-four hours a day," FEMA administrator David Paulison ordered.

When discussing the problem with Jindal at his command briefing, the governor seemed calm but concerned. He listened as FEMA's Bob Fenton laid out the issue, suggesting that the National Guard give out fewer boxes of meals to each car and have people come back in a few days. Jindal encouraged FEMA and state responders to work together to solve the problem. His tone and demeanor suggested a "we, the team" challenge requiring a "we, the team" response.

Minutes after being briefed, Jindal strode into his press conference and gave a blistering summary of the federal government's response to the disaster. FEMA had failed, the governor said, to meet the commodity needs of disaster survivors. He unleashed a torrent of criticism, blaming everything on the agency.

My boss, Marty Bahamonde, told me we had no choice but to respond. Immediately after Jindal's FEMA take-down presser, Marty huddled with several reporters near the podium. He didn't criticize the governor or state, and he acknowledged FEMA's responsibilities, but he also asked for the public's help.

"We need people to be prudent," he said. "Maybe take a little less than a one-week supply. Come back later for more. We're working on improving our supplies and the distribution pipeline."

When Jindal saw Marty's quotes the following day, he seemed especially angry and fired back at his regular evening press conference. I was in the room as he spoke, and this is my perception of his remarks:

How dare FEMA question the integrity of our citizens? Louisianans are not greedy. We need food and water. FEMA needs to improve, get its act together, and bring in these commodities. The federal government has let us down. Our people only take what they need. The federal government has said they're working on meeting our needs. That sounds like the check's in the mail. I'll believe it when I see it.

Whether he was feigning anger or expressing genuine indignation, Jindal let it rip. Mike Byrne's three C's were "commitment, compassion, and courage," but it seemed to me "complex, competent, and calculating" fit Jindal better.

Marty decided my turn had come to give the agency's nightly rejoinder. I asked him what he wanted me to say when the media called to get FEMA's latest reaction to the saga.

"Respond as you see best," he said.

I figured the best strategy at this point was to acknowledge we understood the governor's concern and grasped the gravity of the problem, and to tell them FEMA took responsibility and we were working on a fix.

The next day Marty thanked me for acknowledging the state's concerns. However, he thought my quote was an unusual choice of words for an official spokesperson for the United States Government. I had said, "Wow. The governor slammed us today."

"I don't recall ever hearing a government spokesperson say someone 'slammed us' before," he said. However, I think he agreed that my statement made the point we wanted, which was, "Hey, governor, we hear you, and we know there's a problem."

Semantics aside, there was no question that the need for emergency commodities was real. People were hurting. Mike Hall and Bob Fenton refused to join the governor's blame game. Until crews restored power and stores reopened, people needed food and water, so they focused on solving the distribution problem. "The governor's priorities are our priorities," Hall told his staff.

The National Guard, the Governor's Office of Homeland Security and Emergency Preparedness, and people like the governor's competent disaster point person, Paul Rainwater, worked non-stop on distribution and clearing roads for the power crews. Once the distribution centers overflowed with stock, the governor stopped talking about it.

Contrast that with how an official from another state handled similar problems with commodity distribution after a hurricane, accompanied by complaints from local officials, demands for resignations, and withering media criticism.

"If you want to blame someone, blame me. It's my responsibility. It's the state's responsibility, and I'm State Director. The governor can fire me if he wants to. It's my job to get those supplies to the local community."

The disaster was Hurricane Wilma. The year was 2005. The state was Florida. And the official was the director of the Florida Division of Emergency Management, Craig Fugate.

I remained a fan of Jindal for some of his crisis leadership attributes. He excelled at managing a complex, multi-organization response. Emergency managers continue to study his approach to managing command meetings and copy his style of a priority-centric meeting agenda.

Yet someone I perceive as a well-publicized blamer can damage interagency coordination, communication, and cooperation. Blamers often thrive initially, as the media can confuse a blamer with a fighter. However, calling a blamer a fighter is not a win for the disaster. Nor is it a win for survivors.

Ten Reasons "Blamers" Shift Blame

1. They don't want survivors to blame them for the disaster.
2. They don't understand how disaster response works and criticize other organizations for what they are responsible for doing.
3. It works. It can be a short-term winning strategy—if your goal is to protect your name and reputation.
4. They sincerely believe they're helping and that being critical is the best way to galvanize others. They may think *and sometimes be correct* that response agencies haven't grasped how big the disaster is.
5. They fall in love with the publicity they've garnered and are afraid to correct or adjust their initial message. Their negativity made them famous, and now their reputation has trapped them. They fear that if they change their message, they'll lose credibility.
6. They're a prop for, or have, a political agenda separate from the immediate disaster.
7. They don't know how to work within the emergency management system to raise concerns. Or, they don't trust this system to respond to their problems, so they go around it.

8. They are covering up their screw-ups or their fear of responsibility. They think the disaster is too big and that they can't handle it.
9. They're echoing the complaints they've heard others make.
10. They think that's what leaders do.

Blamers might win the public relations battle in the short term, but "winning" is relative. They are treading water. They won't sink below the crisis, but they will never rise above it.

For one thing, blaming others slows the recovery. Leaders who choose to blame lose three things vital for advancing through a crisis: trust, participation, and momentum. Among your team, confidence fades, participation dissipates, and momentum stalls. Public recrimination of crisis leaders by other crisis leaders does not solve problems. Rather, it damages the cooperation needed to solve them.

The public may also wonder if this deflection hides insecurity or incompetence, causing them to question the blamer's potential as a leader. It may not even be an obvious observation. Sometimes the negativity just sticks with the blamer, like dandruff they can't wash away. People don't feel hopeful or confident about their leadership, even if they're unsure of why.

Name one leader from any disaster of any significance or any world historical crisis who employed the blame game, inspired people to great things, and eventually became revered and admired for their leadership. I can't think of one. However, I can name many who rallied communities and nations during tough times by using public statements to motivate survivors, recognize accomplishments, set honest expectations about challenges, embrace responsibility, and foster teamwork.

This is not to say crisis leaders should avoid challenging assumptions, pointing out mistakes, allowing intense debate, and listening to different opinions. All of that is essential to the internal crisis management process. The key word is *internal*. Public proclamations about who should be blamed for the problem of the day are counter productive.

As a new emergency manager, getting caught up in the blame game is easy, especially when everyone seems to be doing it. The more people trust, believe in, and work with our nation's emergency management system, the better the system works. Direct your efforts to strengthen the public's trust in it.

Deepwater Horizon—It's Never Too Late to Adjust

There are three rules at play during every disaster. One, all disasters are local. Two, all politics are local. And three, all disasters are political.

During the Obama administration, the first disaster of national significance was not the catastrophic hurricane the White House staff had been preparing for, but the 2010 Deepwater Horizon spill, which began on April 20.

Apparently taken by surprise, the administration's poor initial response also seemed to be hampered by a challenge all fledgling political administrations face: changing from fighting a crisis with words to tackling it with action. In other words, they hadn't shifted from the promoting and defending crisis-communications posture employed while running *against* the government to executing survivor-oriented emergency strategies once they *were* the government.

Brand new emergency management specialists should be aware that it usually takes new administrations time to shift from leading a campaign to leading a government response. With Deepwater Horizon, federal political leadership's communication strategies first inflamed the crisis; then, after a course correction, helped tame it. Importantly, their rapid midcourse correction resulted in a textbook emergency management approach to earning public trust by accepting responsibility, placing response experts in charge, committing resources, and serving the public's information needs during an emergency.

The lessons learned by the administration served them well in subsequent hurricanes, firestorms, floods, and tornados—390 major disaster declarations in all. In addition, based on news reports I read, the Obama administration incorporated many of these hard-earned crisis leadership lessons in the pandemic playbook they passed to the Trump political team during the 2017 transition. However, the new administration went their own way during the 2019–2020 onset of COVID-19.

But during the oil spill, at first, things did not go well.

Right after the spill, the federal government created perceptions that they were minimizing the event, failing to grasp the environmental and economic catastrophe beginning to take shape. Government messaging focused on how much of the oil was being removed—rather than acknowledging the scope of the problem. Everyone could see the spill was expanding more rapidly than it was being contained.

These early messages did little to reassure the public that the government grasped how big the disaster was. As the federal government presented oil collection statistics, television news images showed the oil spreading across the Gulf of Mexico, washing across beaches, infesting swamplands, and contaminating animal habitats.

People thought the government implied they were doing everything they could to manage the situation, but it didn't look that way. That was bad enough in terms of creating unease. Yet I thought the second mistake sent things into a tailspin.

As criticism mounted, political strategists and communicators from the election campaign huddled with the Administration. They seemed to treat the oil spill more as a public relations crisis, rather than an environmental and economic one. They tried to play the blame game. They attempted to deflect responsibility away from the federal government by focusing blame on the responsible party, primarily the energy company British Petroleum (BP).

The Oil Pollution Act of 1990 requires that the responsible party provide funds for damages, cleanup, and removal. The government oversees the cleanup and provides resources when the responsible party doesn't have enough. While "the law requires the responsible party to pay for it and provide equipment," Coast Guard Admiral Thad Allen explained during a May 24, 2010, Deepwater press briefing at the White House that the federal government is "accountable to make sure it gets done." (Note:

In 2014 a US District Court ruled BP primarily responsible for the spill. In 2015, BP agreed to a settlement with Gulf Coast states and the US Department of Justice.)

The administration compounded the misguided decision to play the Blame Game when they picked Interior Secretary Ken Salazar to spearhead the message. "We're going to keep our boot on the neck of BP," said Salazar. Rather than emphasizing the government's role in the cleanup, the communications goal seemed to be: "Don't let this be Obama's Katrina."

This seemingly image-protecting public messaging strategy reflected a lack of response urgency. I thought it hampered efforts to ignite a complete federal response, even as it became evident the spill was an event of historical significance. It generated criticism even by the president's political allies, such as James Carville, a political consultant and Louisiana native. A different former high-ranking federal political official told me, "I never understood the initial hesitancy [by the Administration] to grab hold of this crisis. Heck, Bill Clinton would have been out there in a wetsuit trying to plug the hole himself."

The administration got the message, changed its public posture 180 degrees, and ramped up the response. The president held a May 27 press conference to clear the air: "If you are wondering who is responsible [for managing the cleanup], I take responsibility," he said. "It took us too long" to acknowledge the scope of the spill.

Coast Guard Commandant Thad Allen, trusted by federal political leaders and well-respected along the Gulf Coast for boosting the faltering response to Hurricane Katrina in 2005, was the president's point person in the reshaped response. Allen prominently emerged as the federal interagency operations lead for the cleanup and became the primary national spokesperson, even appearing at the White House Press Briefing Room. (Allen remained the National Incident Commander for the oil spill an additional three months after he retired from the Coast Guard on June 30, 2010).

In addition to Allen, other high-ranking officials throughout the federal government spoke to the public and provided public and environmental health and economic recovery information. They matched words with actions—not by promising a national response, but by describing the robust and unified private sector and federal response now on the scene.

When crisis leaders respond to events, particularly those in the scope of a Deepwater Horizon or a Katrina, they have to "adapt their mental models, create unity of effort, and lead from everywhere," Admiral Allen told the *Harvard Business Review* in late 2010.

Thinking you can work your way out of the crisis with words doesn't work. You have to solve the situation with action when you're in charge. If you start in the wrong direction, don't keep driving. Adjust and get the response back on track.

HIDE FROM THE PROBLEM.

Hiders think they can message, ignore, or spin their way out of taking charge. Yet if you can help or have a resource that can, you have a responsibility to not withhold those services.

Crisis Implosion in Flint, Michigan

For nearly two years after lead began infiltrating the city's drinking water in 2014, state leaders distanced themselves from the crisis by deferring responsibility and minimizing health concerns. By early 2016, their strategy to avoid owning the situation crumbled in a wave of documentation, negative publicity, recriminations, and resignations.

Consider this summarized excerpt from January 20, 2016, in the *New York Times*:

> A top aide to Michigan's governor referred to people raising questions about the quality of Flint's water as an "anti-everything group." Worrisome findings about lead by a concerned pediatrician were dismissed as "data," in quotes.

> That view of how the administration of Gov. Rick Snyder initially dealt with the water crisis in the city of Flint emerged from emails made public by the governor. The correspondence records complaints by the public and local officials, as well as irritation by state officials over the reluctance to accept their assurances.

> It was not until late in 2015, that state officials finally conceded that Flint was in the midst of a major public health emergency. The emails were released after Mr. Snyder's (2016) State of the State address in which he apologized to the residents of Flint and promised to help remedy the problem.

> Though Mr. Snyder issued the emails to reveal the administration's transparency on the matter, the documents provide a glimpse of state leaders who were at times dismissive of the concerns of residents, seemed eager to place responsibility with local government

and, even as the scientific testing was hinting at a larger problem, were reluctant to acknowledge it.

In January 2021, Michigan's attorney general's office accused Snyder, former Flint emergency manager Darnell Earley, and several other officials of crimes related to the water crisis, including the dissemination of misleading information. Synder in 2021 pleaded not guilty to his two misdemeanor charges of willful neglect of duty. Earley also denied wrongdoing (pleaded not guilty) to three counts of misconduct in office. As of March 2022, legal proceedings against Synder and Earley, along with other criminal and civil cases related to the water crisis, were continuing through the court system.

Hiders are experts at deferring, denying, deflecting, distancing, disengaging, disappearing, distracting, dodging, or dismissing. If you can sum up your leader's crisis response with one of these words beginning with d, you've probably got a hider.

If you have a public health and safety responsibility, whether that's a legal responsibility or one assumed by the authority of your position, you cannot hide from the crisis. Eventually, the situation will find you and drag you right in.

OWN THE PROBLEM

One day, I got a call from a local health care administrator who insisted I meet with some of her clients from the disabled community whom responders had evacuated after a disaster. "They have some important things to tell you," she said.

"No way," I thought. I saw myself in the hot seat, hammered

with a barrage of complaints and requests to fix things I had no control over. I begged off, but she persisted. I finally caved and went to the meeting.

I sat around a table with about ten clients, all of whom had some form of severe disability. One woman was separated from her comfort dog during the flood and cried as she recounted her experience. A young guy, who must have been 6'4" and weighed 270 pounds, had a mental disability. He told me that when he gets scared, he becomes angry and can't control it. The evacuation happened so fast he panicked and started waving his arms, threatening people, and yelling.

"They tied me down and locked me up," he said. "It was like living in a nightmare."

When everyone finished telling their stories, my advocate friend began the second part of the agenda. "Now, let's talk about what we need to do next time," she said.

I thought, *Here it comes. I get to hear what we need to do better.*

I was surprised, big time. Not one person in the room asked for anything. No one told me what emergency management needed to do for them. Instead, every one of them told me what they had done to help emergency managers.

The guy who got tied down kept a piece of paper with him with his sister's phone numbers on it. "I have a plan now," he said. "I say call her, and she'll come and get me."

The woman with the dog now carried a doctor's note saying she needed the pet for comfort and reassurance. Others in the room maintained extra doses of prescription medicine tucked away in their go kits. They all carried emergency contact numbers and had prepared notes with special instructions to hand to their rescuers in case of an emergency.

"We wanted you to know what we're doing to help our first responders," they said at the end of the meeting.

One of the things former FEMA administrator Craig Fugate stressed was the importance of responsibility in a crisis. He challenged individuals to think differently about their role and emergency managers to think differently about the people they served.

"In a disaster," he said, "the public is an asset, not a liability."

The more people do on their own in a crisis, the less governments, the private sector, and voluntary organizations need to do for them. Public involvement frees rescuers and resources to concentrate on the most critical needs, like searching for those trapped in collapsed structures, fighting back floodwaters, treating the injured, or sheltering the newly homeless. By leveraging the public as part of the response team, disaster coordinators can expand their capacity to help.

The 1997 Grand Forks Flood

Former Federal Coordinating Officer, Lesli Rucker, recalls the night North Dakota's Adjutant General, Major General Keith Bjerke, returned to the statewide command center in Bismarck to brief responders on the Grand Forks flood fight late in the evening on April 18, 1997. When Lesli last spoke with him, flood fighters remained hopeful they could save the city.

City workers, citizens, the US Army Corps of Engineers, and the National Guard lined atop the levees shoulder to shoulder. They fought to beat back the rising Red River of the North by erecting miles of emergency protection lines. In early April, Hannah, the eighth blizzard of the season, had hammered them, freezing sandbags and snapping power lines.

Under lights powered by generators, thousands of people piled sandbags, dug up back yards for extra dirt, passed out food and water, and built second lines of defense in the city's interior. Schools were closed, and the University of North Dakota canceled classes to throw more people at the flood.

Even during the fight, outside observers, community members, and critics through the media pointed out reasons for the looming disaster. They raised questions about the strategies used to fight the flood and even the accuracy of the forecast.

On April 4th, the river reached flood stage at twenty-eight feet. Based on the National Weather Service prediction, flood fighters widely assumed the flood peak would be forty-nine feet. On April 18, when all hell began to break loose, the river had risen to 52.62 feet, climbing eighteen inches in eighteen hours. The final peak hit 54.35 feet on April 22.

In the state's command center in Bismarck, Bjerke called the team together. He didn't address any of the blame for the disaster. In a quiet voice, he told them, "Grand Forks fought this thing. Everyone did. They've lost the flood fight. They're evacuating the city."

Lesli remembers the room went still in disbelief. "You could hear a pin drop," she said.

After a moment, Bjerke refocused the room. "They'll come back. And we're going to help them."

"Owning" in emergency management means a relentless commitment to interagency and intergovernmental team building. You share credit and public praise when it is warranted. You create an environment where organizations feel encouraged to take risks, knowing you won't throw them under the bus. Often, when you shoulder responsibility this way during a crisis, you galvanize others to join you. People want to be on your team.

Patricia "Pat" Owens, mayor of Grand Forks, North Dakota, counted on the help Bjerke promised. Before becoming mayor herself, Owens served as an executive assistant for the Mayor's office for thirty-three years. In 1996, she ran herself—and won, to the surprise of some. She had been in office less than a year when the Red River flooded, and Grand Forks suffered the worst disaster in the state's history, as well as one of the most significant disasters ever recorded in the US "The worst flood to befall an American city until Katrina," the Louisiana news outlet NOLA.com later reported.

When Grand Forks lost their flood fight, water from the overtopped levees swamped the city. Then, as floodwaters peaked, a fire broke out and destroyed a large part of downtown. The water was too deep for fire trucks to get there without being hoisted onto military trucks to keep them above the flooded streets.

When levees fail, the water not only floods the town, but it also often remains there for a period of time. The same levees built to hold the water out now hold it in like a bathtub. Once inside the community, water doesn't stop moving. It flows on, searching for an outlet, carrying remnants of homes, cars, and personal belongings along the way. Sometimes, the water drains out naturally once the outside level recedes. But often, flood waters continue to circle inside homes until homeowners can pump the water out.

As mayor, Owens chose to own the recovery effort. "Keep the faith" became her signature advice to struggling homeowners and businesses.

"It's not going to be easy, and it will take time," she said, "but we can, and we will recover." She became the face of the community as the country watched.

Her attitude attracted help beyond the people in the state. While driving through Lincoln Park, a neighborhood so hard hit and vulnerable to future floods that it would never be rebuilt, her cell phone rang. President Clinton asked how the recovery was going and requested her first-hand assessment of his federal agencies on the scene.

After seeing Owens on television, McDonald's hamburger chain heir Joan Kroc donated $15 million to the recovery. Then-US Department of Housing and Urban Development Secretary Andrew Cuomo dispatched a top aide to the city to present

Grand Forks with a $50 million Community Development Block Grant. During the press conference announcement for the grant, Mayor Owens thanked all the people and organizations supporting the city.

She thanked HUD, of course, but also the governor and state emergency management, her staff, the North Dakota congressional delegation, the National Guard, volunteers from throughout the country, the people of Grand Forks, James Lee Witt and FEMA... On and on she went, thanking everyone she considered part of the team.

I arrived in Grand Forks on April 20 to manage a federal satellite field office. Standing in the back of the briefing room that day, I remembered feeling like I would have run through a brick wall for Mayor Owens and the entire community. And I'm sure most of my colleagues felt the same way. Owens shared her criticisms and frustrations in private and offered merited praise in public. Her goals were simple. It was her responsibility to get the city as much help as possible. To do that, she needed an interagency, intergovernmental, and private sector team that trusted one another. A group that felt encouraged to take chances, test ideas, and explore creative initiatives. Some ideas worked, and some didn't, but never once was anyone unjustly blamed.

THROWING YOURSELF INTO THE FRAY

No disaster response goes perfectly, and Grand Forks was no exception. Three months after the levees failed, a prominent city official appeared at an international hazards conference. In front of hundreds of community leaders and emergency managers, he said the federal government had failed to respond to the community's needs. "We told FEMA we needed a lifeline to survive," he said, "and they handed us a piece of rope."

Mayor Owens wasn't happy. She reached out to FEMA director James Lee Witt to let him know the negative comments did not reflect her leadership team's belief. She offered to contact every attendee at the conference to set the record straight.

Unfortunately, her city representative wasn't the only critic. Around the same time, an East Coast publication ran a series of articles describing the growing anger and frustration in Grand Forks. A community influencer promoted the phrase "Uff-Dah FEMA," a Scandinavian-American expression that could mean anything from exasperation to something more.

A neighborhood organizer asked me to round up FEMA staff for a public dunking booth "to help people express their grievances with the agency." I had heard the complaints, too, but there was no way I would allow our professional recovery workers to be humiliated as floundering game show contestants. "We'll increase our face-to-face outreach in the neighborhoods instead," I said. In addition to the other complaints, congressional members weighed in, questioning the federal commitment as the disaster faded from the national headlines.

Even with strong local leadership, every disaster recovery hits a rough patch after agencies have met immediate needs, and the community begins to confront longer-term and more complicated recovery challenges.

Grand Forks wasn't a run-of-the-mill recovery operation. The city needed to rebuild the entire community. As criticism mounted, there was concern it might be a tipping point, damaging the intergovernmental relations the town had worked so hard to build. As strong as our nation's emergency management system was at that time, it depended on intergovernmental trust. Lose that faith, and you have lost the disaster.

North Dakota Governor Ed Schafer, who was notably a Republican while a Democrat occupied the White House, charged into the fray. He did not have to jump in. No one was criticizing his team. Under the response leadership of General Bjerke and the state director of emergency management Doug Friez, the state of North Dakota had received good marks.

Rather than joining the critics, however, Schafer challenged popular assumptions. During public appearances and in a separate op-ed, he talked about the importance of partnership and the value of working together. He praised the intergovernmental team and went out of his way to thank the federal government and FEMA.

Schafer's timely support shored up relationships among responding agencies and was vital to keeping the recovery moving forward. The governor refocused everyone on pushing forward together rather than defending themselves. It meant a lot to federal relief workers to hear that the governor had their back.

A BUNCH OF OWNERS

Owning up also means giving your critics the benefit of the doubt. You're not afraid to ask, "What if they're right?" You want to bring onboard anyone who can help improve the response.

Leaders who take ownership will analyze a problem by asking three questions:

1. Do we have an operational problem (for example, an overlooked community or underestimated need for water)?
2. Do we have an emergency information problem (for example, confusing people about the assistance process)?
3. Do we have an interagency or intergovernmental relationship problem? Is this critic raising issues we can work with them to solve?

Pay attention to how leaders respond to disasters through live or television appearances, and practice identifying if they are a Blamer, a Hider, or an Owner. Examples will be everywhere.

"Sounds like a drinking game," one emergency manager told me when I shared this advice. "The first one to identify the choice gets to drink. As long as you're not deployed, of course."

By taking responsibility, you demonstrate leadership. The more you show leadership, the more opportunities you will be given for significant emergency management projects, initiatives, and positions.

Masters of this principle are grateful for the chance to own something in a crisis and see it as an opportunity to make a difference. If you can do this, you are well on your way to being a leader for the emerging generation.

What's more, the earlier in your career you embrace the principle of owning up, the more decisive you will become as a leader. However, this choice comes with difficulties. People may blame you for things outside your control. That, too, comes with the act of owning.

When you wonder how crisis teams you admire can rise to the occasion and function seamlessly, this is often the reason why. They have a bunch of owners.

During your emergency management career, you'll likely face similar ownership choices—and be in a position to advise others, as well. It's not a bad idea to anticipate such a decision point. Evaluate the options, consider the consequences, and think through how you'll react.

CHAPTER 5

Promote the Dog Sitter

HOW TO BE AN INDEPENDENT THINKER

"However beautiful the strategy, you should occasionally look at the results."

—WINSTON CHURCHILL

A search and rescue team heads out to Left Hand Canyon near Boulder, Colorado during the state's 2013 flood disaster. Photo by Michael Rieger/FEMA.

They had left the sleeping bags outside, along with tents, coverings, bottled water, meals-ready-to-eat (MREs), and cooking utensils. Boxes and camping supplies were getting ruined, spread across a rain-soaked, sunken concrete lot behind the US Embassy in Haiti.

Darryl Madden directed the SUV he had requisitioned from the motor pool over to the edge of the pile. He tossed damp boxes in the cargo hold and stuffed rumpled pup tents across the seats. He was going to give what few supplies he could pack to the earthquake survivors and had roped me in to help.

We'd arrived three weeks earlier as part of the US humanitarian relief effort for the magnitude 7.0 earthquake that struck Haiti on January 20, 2010. According to the United Nations, the disaster killed approximately 220,000 people and injured 300,0000 more. Imagine if the entire population of a Des Moines, Iowa, or Birmingham, Alabama perished on a single day due to a natural disaster.

Among Haiti's civilian workforce, sixteen thousand public servants died, and the earthquake destroyed almost all government buildings. After two decades in emergency response, it was the deadliest disaster I had worked.

Weeks after the earthquake, we found a family of elementary-school-aged orphans living in the rubble. There were piles of bodies collected by front-end loaders scattered everywhere.

Darryl recalls working with the search and rescue teams. "A week after the earthquake, you could hear people trapped under the concrete. You could hear them tapping."

He connected with fifteen families at the end of a neighborhood on a hill in Port-au-Prince. Many were living in the remnants of their former dwellings. The survivors included children taking care of younger siblings after the earthquake killed their parents.

Emergency managers often "adopt" a family or small neighborhood after a disaster. They'll follow them through the aftermath, because it provides insights into the entire event.

A few weeks after the earthquake, the search phase of the response ended, and the US rescue teams departed. The teams were all part of FEMA's national urban search and rescue system. We knew them and had worked with them on other disasters.

When the teams departed Haiti, they left their billeting supply cache behind. National search teams arrive at disasters self-sufficient, so as not to burden local responders. They typically leave gear to support an ongoing response and because it's cheaper to repurchase new supplies than ship back disaster-racked tents. Before they left, the teams asked us to donate some of their used camping equipment to earthquake survivors.

"Do us a solid," they'd said. "Grab what you need. Give away what you can. Don't let this stuff sit here, get picked apart by people who don't need it, or end up in the trash. We know it's not much, but maybe it'll help a few families."

As Daryl and I began assessing the supplies and preparing them for donation, a voice behind us yelled, "What the hell are you doing?"

We looked up to see a contract employee for one of the lead

agencies for US Haiti earthquake relief. She was one of our bosses, though she rarely appeared at staff meetings and hadn't spoken to us in weeks. We thought she didn't like us much, and as a result, we didn't like her either.

"What are you doing with that equipment?" she demanded.

"We're taking it to a local neighborhood," Madden told her. "You know we got the okay."

"Put it back. I'll take care of that donation for them later."

"Look at all the stuff left. This is nothing. Besides, the rain's ruining it. Come on. You know people are really hurting out there."

"Put it all back, or I'm reporting you. I don't care what you thought your assignment was. We have a new process for this donation."

"What are you talking about?" Darryl asked, but she didn't answer.

My head was spinning, trying to figure out what was right. Unpleasant though this person was, she was still a supervisor, and one reputedly with White House connections. I was cognizant of our FEMA support role to her organization. We weren't in charge. Still, we had been tasked to donate, we weren't misappropriating anything, and we had promised the USAR teams. Slowly, I started to unload the boxes.

Darryl looked at me, shook his head and rolled his eyes, signaling it was an empty threat. He stared at her and didn't move.

Appearing frustrated, the woman glanced up at the rain. She glared at us, then dashed back into the embassy. Once she was out of sight, Darryl reloaded everything I had just unpacked. "Ridiculous," he muttered to himself.

Thirty minutes later, we unpacked again, this time at Darryl's adopted neighborhood. We never heard another word about our donation mission, not from the supervisor who'd confronted us, our other bosses in Haiti, or anyone else. She seemingly had invented a roadblock on the spot. It seemed to me she wanted to play a bureaucratic control game. I didn't see that at the time, but Darryl did.

A decade later, Darryl vividly remembers that day.

"One of my personal proudest moments," he said about the encounter. "Just the right thing to do. You find out who you are in those moments. Maybe we would have gotten in trouble. Send me home if that's what you want, but I'm going to do this."

Darryl had instinctively checked all the decision boxes, as we had been taught when faced with a crisis dilemma. Morally, legally, ethically, and assignment-wise, it was the right thing to do for Haiti. Earthquake survivors got equipment that was going to be ruined or thrown away. We put the supplies to good use in a bad situation.

I'd admired Darryl for years. After this episode, my respect for him skyrocketed. He dared to be survivor-centric. He could spot what I thought was a fake power play. He knew what rules mattered and had an inner compass to determine right from wrong. He was an independent thinker.

GO ALONG TO GET ALONG

Most people in emergency management work for the government at one time or another. That is where most of the jobs are, especially if you are just starting. At various points in my federal career, I've heard from senior employees:

"Don't put your head up because someone can chop it off."

"Lay low, be average. Don't try to be great because then you'll get too much work."

"Wait until someone tells you what to do, and don't do anything until headquarters tells you what they want."

In other words, if I wanted a long career and future promotions, I had to go along to get along. I've known people who have done well with this advice. While they were fantastic bureaucrats, it made them horrible disaster responders.

Government work tends to attract, and often reward, risk-avoiders. Yet crisis response work demands risk-takers. Therefore, a big part of an emergency management job is learning to be a risk-taker in a risk-averse environment.

Independent thinking sometimes requires that you put your reputation on the line. As the always-quotable Craig Fugate said when he ran FEMA, "When disasters strike: Think Big, Go Big, Go Fast, Go Smart. And if you need to leave one out, forget smart."

PLAY IT WITH ARROGANCE

In emergency management, arrogance is not being an obnoxious jerk. It means being willing to face down adversity, question assumptions, and embrace the opportunity. It means having the quiet conviction to think for yourself. In the 1998 baseball movie, *Bull Durham*, veteran catcher Crash Davis tells rookie pitcher Ebby Calvin Laloosh, "You gotta play this game with fear and arrogance. Even when you're getting beat." That's not bad advice for emergency managers, either.

Every disaster poses unpredictable and unprecedented challenges. In the response phase, no one knows everything. More often, no one knows anything. Rather than focusing on getting your questions answered, practice adapting to the curveballs.

SEVEN WAYS TO BECOME AN INDEPENDENT THINKER

Independent thinking is an essential skill in this profession. You don't get an instruction manual on how to handle every conceivable scenario you'll face during a disaster. To help you understand how crisis leaders develop and demonstrate the principle of independent thinking, I've included seven techniques to build your skills, along with examples.

1. Know what, ask why.
2. Consider the art of laziness.
3. Recognize the exception/never underestimate anybody.
4. Challenge conventional wisdom.
5. Be survivor-centric.
6. Draw your conclusions.
7. Know the difference between rules and tools.

Lesli Rucker was the first woman in emergency management appointed by the President as a Federal Coordinating Officer for a catastrophic disaster. She was a big advocate of encouraging her staff to be independent thinkers when she worked for FEMA.

Her advice was, "Know what the problem is. We would hear this a lot during a disaster: 'We need more stuff.' But what's the right stuff?" She suggested asking yourself two questions:

1. Why do you need this?
2. What problem are we trying to solve?

To illustrate, she told me about the time she ran a federal flood recovery disaster, and her operations director walked in and plopped a request on her desk.

"This concerns me," he said. "Are we missing something?"

A local emergency operations center had requested that FEMA send them an epidemiologist. There was no other background or explanation, just a request for the medical professional marked Urgent.

Lesli knew she had to deal with the request right away. Public health issues go to the top of the priority pile. Yet something gnawed at her. Why hadn't she heard rumblings of this before? Was it the tip of an emerging public health problem or simply a misdirected request?

"Sit down," she told her operations director.

Lesli called her counterpart at the governor's office, who had no further information. Together they patched in the county's emergency manager and asked those two questions. Why do you need this? And what problem are we trying to solve?

They discovered the request had originated from the public inquiry section at the local EOC. Residents had questions about cleaning up mold, which the call takers didn't have the expertise to answer.

They didn't need an epidemiologist to treat illnesses. The problem was a lack of public information to prevent people from becoming sick.

Lesli suggested getting pamphlets on cleaning up mold from the CDC, coordinating that messaging with the county health department, and having the community relations teams distribute the material door to door. Problem solved.

Ask Why. It Can Be a Matter of Life and Death

During evacuations, responders often encourage the public to check on friends, neighbors, and family to relieve the burden on overwhelmed front-line responders.

However, this advice does not make sense in all disasters. Agencies use it before hurricanes when residents have days to get ready. You would never issue this guidance during a flash flood when people may only have seconds to get to safety.

In 1996, I managed a documentary project commemorating the twenty-year remembrance of Colorado's Big Thompson Canyon

Flood, which killed 144 people. We talked to one rescuer who recalled standing near a bridge as a wall of water two stories high rushed down the narrow canyon, carrying hundreds of cars, many with their lights on and families inside.

One well-meaning federal employee failed to consider this kind of distinction among incidents. During a raging wildfire, this emergency management specialist tweeted on behalf of the government, "Check on your neighbors before you evacuate to make sure they don't need help."

Again, it's hard to overstate the danger of this advice. People have died in wildfires because they took a few seconds to dash back into their homes to retrieve a wallet from the kitchen counter. Luckily, we quickly caught the tweet and got it deleted from the agency's feed.

While checking on neighbors is an excellent message during many disasters, it's not a hard-and-fast rule for all of them. This employee thought he was doing what FEMA headquarters wanted. He was on autopilot. He didn't think about why the message existed. He should have asked himself, *Why am I sending this? Does it help front-line responders? Does it keep people safe?* Obviously, the answers are no.

CONSIDER THE ART OF LAZINESS

I once asked an emergency manager I admired who he admired as a crisis leader. He suggested I read up on Admiral Raymond Spruance, who oversaw the decisive US victory at Midway during World War II. Many historians credit his command decisions during the battle as one of the most impressive demonstrations of leadership in Naval history.

I came across an interview where the reporter probed for insights on his leadership style. Spruance told him, "I'm lazy."

Spruance wasn't lazy in the ordinary sense. He had extraordinary self-discipline, didn't smoke, and rarely drank alcohol, preferring hot chocolate. During the planning for Midway, he often walked up to ten miles a day.

Spruance valued the time spent uncluttering his mind. To free up time, he delegated and did not micromanage tactical details. He didn't require that his staff bring him every decision they made.

Other officers described him as patient, quiet, modest, and self-effacing. They considered him a brilliant planner. I believe he gave equal attention to reserving his energy. He concentrated on being ready for the few big decisions determining the battle's outcome.

Emergency managers tend to be type-A personalities, jam-packing their days planning projects and meetings. We have been described as such adrenaline junkies that if we don't have an actual crisis, we'll create one just to feel the rush of having something urgent to occupy our time. The downside, of course, is burnout and missed opportunities. Like Spruance, sometimes the best thing you can do is absolutely nothing.

Don't read emails. Don't draw up another to-do list. Go outside, walk around, or sit at your desk and stare into space. On occasion, flat-out *be lazy*.

"Some people believe that when I am quiet that I am thinking some deep and important thoughts," Spruance told his interviewer. "The fact is that I'm thinking nothing at all. My mind is blank."

In a 2012 scientific study published in *Consciousness and Cognition*, researchers concluded, "data indicate [that] minimal attention…engages processes associated with the management of successful long-term goals." In other words, consider the value of laziness. Shake the cobwebs from your head. You might be amazed how some seemingly complex issues suddenly become more manageable.

RECOGNIZE THE EXCEPTION

While studying Admiral Spruance, I discovered another fascinating historical figure who contributed to the victory at Midway. Commander Joseph Rochefort ran a team of cryptanalysts and linguists as part of the Navy's intelligence for the US Pacific fleet. He helped crack the Japanese code used to communicate their operational plans.

In addition to brilliant analytical skills, Rochefort was notable for his appearance. He didn't look like a recruitment poster for a naval officer. In the basement of the building where he worked with his code breakers, he wore a kimono over his uniform and bedroom slippers. That didn't matter to the command staff at Pearl Harbor. All they cared about was whether he could help win the war.

You will find Joseph Rocheforts everywhere in emergency management. One of them might even be you. They are the ones who don't always function smoothly within the daily office routine. You almost have to tie them down to keep them in place. Yet when disaster strikes, they can be magic when let loose in an environment where they can be their best.

In 1995, FEMA hired Ronnie Jones, an elk hunting guide from Colorado. Every time we called, he would show up with his big smile, mountain twang, and wearing a FEMA hat that never seemed to fit right on his mop of hair. When we first hired him, I pigeonholed him in outreach to rural areas. In my mind, he looked the part.

Ken Jordan, who ran our community relations program at the time, soon told me I underestimated him.

"He connects with people," Ken said. "Not just the hunting and fishing crowd."

We ran low on staff and desperately needed someone to liaise with a good-sized city on one occasion. We turned to Ronnie, who showed up on every disaster if called.

The city officials loved him. He did a great job on the assignment. After that, we used him everywhere, even tossing him into the bustle of New York City following Superstorm Sandy. Ronnie, who died in 2018, received some of his highest praise from urban areas. He connected quickly with people in disasters because he was honest and kind, he spoke straight, and he knew the agency's programs.

People are often written off, overlooked, or underestimated for various reasons. They don't have a big name, the right look, or a meaningful title. But don't count them out. One of the most rewarding things about emergency management is seeing people unexpectedly step up and do something great.

CHALLENGE CONVENTIONAL WISDOM

Craig Fugate became nationally known for crisis leadership after managing the response to four back-to-back-to-back-to-back hurricanes that hit Florida in 2004 when he was Governor Jeb Bush's point person for emergencies.

In 2009, newly-inaugurated President Obama appointed him FEMA administrator. The President tasked Fugate with rebuilding the nation's disaster management system, which had fumbled during Hurricane Katrina.

People everywhere praised the appointment of Fugate, a hurricane response expert. Conventional wisdom concluded that hurricanes obviously should be the nation's number-one disaster priority—look at Katrina. Fugate, however, had a different point of view, which he made clear at his introductory meeting with the emergency management community.

"Stop focusing only on hurricanes," he told a packed auditorium and national video audience of responders. "Our next disaster could be an earthquake. We're FEMA, not HEMA—the Hurricane Emergency Management Agency. We're all hazards, all the time. As of right now, we start planning smart. That means we stop planning as if the next disaster will be exactly like the last disaster."

Fugate challenged conventional wisdom by doing the opposite of what everyone expected. In 2009, most of the country assumed FEMA would focus on a Katrina replica. Many of us took away from his remarks that day a commonsensical but still eye-opening perspective on disaster planning. It's too late to prepare for a disaster that's already happened. Instead of preparing for the last big disaster, prepare for the next big disaster, which could happen anytime, anywhere, and be anything.

In season five of the comedy television series *Seinfeld*, (1989–1998) George concludes that his life is a mess because every instinct he has is wrong. He starts doing the opposite of what he would typically do, and his life dramatically—and hilariously—improves.

When companies, schools, and other government facilities close due to an impending disaster, that's when emergency managers open their EOCs. Doing the opposite of everyone else is sort of our thing.

BE SURVIVOR-CENTRIC

Independent thinkers in this field recognize that it can be challenging to remain survivor-focused in a disaster. They are constantly on guard against being pulled away from what's essential: thinking about the people they serve.

During an exercise to practice how the nation would respond to a catastrophic California earthquake, moderators asked a senior federal official what his priorities would be. Without hesitation, he said, "Be busy with the White House and DHS headquarters. They'll need information, and we want to make sure we meet their needs."

Now, none of you are naïve. You need to feed the beast above. Not doing that will invite micromanagement and unwanted interference in the operation. What's more, the organizations above you have an essential role in establishing policies, endorsing priorities, and ensuring you have the resources to respond. It is part of your job to keep them informed, and it should be a priority. Yet I question whether it should have been the priority. It certainly should not have been the only priority.

Priority number one should always be survivor-centric. For example, "We're going to do everything it takes to assist the State of California with communications so earthquake survivors have access to emergency aid and can start applying for disaster financial assistance"—or—"We're going to support the front-line responders with transportation resources so they can keep saving lives."

We all can fall into the trap of thinking first, and sometimes only, of the people far above us in the organization. To paraphrase personal finance author, businessman, and radio show host David Ramsey, "During a crisis, don't seek approvals that you don't need, using time you can't spare, to please people you don't serve." (*Ramsey said: "We buy things we don't need with money we don't have to impress people we don't like."*)

In 2010, Hurricane Earl became the hurricane that didn't strike. FEMA staged disaster response teams in thirteen states in preparation for the monster storm. Fortunately, Earl swerved out to sea before hitting the East Coast. After a few days of waiting for the all-clear, the teams went home. I had deployed with the group sent to Connecticut.

Before we left, I ran into a newly-minted disaster response expert who had just joined the agency, a political appointee fresh from the outside world. He exuded confidence when I found him in the parking lot before a wrap-up meeting with the governor at the state operations center.

He was on the phone reading aloud a gushing newspaper column that praised the agency for its rapid action in advance of the hurricane. He held up one finger, motioning for to me to hold on while he finished his call. Though no disaster materialized, the column suggested FEMA would have been ready if one had. The fact that the agency had sent thirteen teams to the East Coast seemed a marvelous feat and indicative of a new, better, post-Katrina federal agency in the eye of the journalist.

"Can you believe this?" the guy kept saying to the person on the other end of his call as he read line after line of editorial kudos. He was giddy with excitement. It was as if FEMA—with him now part of it—had just conquered Katrina, burying the ghost of that failure forever.

He wrapped up the conversation, pocketed his phone, and looked at me.

"Can you believe this?" he asked.

"But we didn't do anything," I said. "We sat around for a few days watching The Weather Channel and collecting Marriott reward points. And now we're going home."

He shot me a withering look. "It's still really good," he said.

FEMA's operations leadership later slammed the door on the premature excitement of this political gunner and other agency newbies like him, who had yet to work an actual disaster.

"That wasn't a disaster," they said. "It was a drill. Stop patting yourselves on the back. We did nothing. We helped no one."

Inexperienced crisis leaders often fall in love with positive press clippings. They crave validation from good-looking, articulate public commentators who talk about the news on TV. While it's much nicer to get positive press than the negative kind, sometimes it is best ignored.

Several months into recovery from the 2013 Colorado Floods, a network news anchor said, "We checked back in with local leaders in Colorado, and not one of them had anything bad to say about FEMA."

Most people in the agency ignored the clip. It seemed like a throwaway line without much context. Thanks to the heavy lifting of recovery work by local leaders, the state, and volunteers—none of whom the newscaster mentioned—the disaster was going well.

One federal official, however, thought this slight praise was fantastic. He sent the anchor's quote to everyone working the disaster: "Look who's saying wonderful things about us. Excellent job, everyone!"

He thought the news network's praise would mean as much to everyone else as it did to him, but the effort fell flat. The manager's note sounded overeager for recognition and showed misplaced trust in whose feedback mattered. It wasn't survivor-centric. It was media-centric.

Emergency managers occasionally get frustrated with negative news, peers' criticism, legislators' challenges, and second-guessing from self-appointed crisis expert spectators. It would be best if you avoided the tendency to look for praise constantly. Specifically, watch out if you're responding to a crisis by:

1. asking, "What does my headquarters want me to do?" or
2. concluding, "I must be doing a good job because we're getting good press."

If you study exceptional leaders, you'll notice these aren't questions they ask or metrics they value. They'd rather know: have we implemented operational plans and achieved results?

The goal isn't to get media accolades, please critics, or seek pats on the back. It is to help survivors and recovering communities. We do that by relieving suffering, stabilizing the situation, cleaning up the mess, and creating partnerships for recovery.

If you see these goals out of order, do the opposite.

DRAW YOUR CONCLUSIONS

Often, lessons learned from a disaster may not be what everyone else assumes. When you dig deeper, you find nuggets of insights that may help you in the future.

Public commentators and academics have employed the

"Brownie" story to describe what they believe went wrong during Hurricane Katrina, as if the collapse of the entire national emergency management system was the apparent fault of one person. Sometimes, they'll say the word to draw a laugh or get applause.

"Brownie" is the nickname President George Bush gave Mike Brown, the director of FEMA at that time.

"Brownie, you're doing a heck of a job," Bush said while visiting an Air National Guard base seven days after the storm. Yet less than a week later, as the response in Louisiana further morphed into chaos, the White House recalled Brown to Washington, DC and relieved him of his Katrina role as Principal Federal Official. Three days later, Brown resigned as FEMA director.

The media widely used the president's compliment to juxtapose images of people at the New Orleans Superdome without food, water, or medical care and corpses floating in floodwaters above the city's streets. It conveyed the message that the federal government was both incompetent and disengaged from the realities of the disaster.

Yet you will rarely, if ever, hear veteran emergency management professionals utter the phrase "Brownie" in this context. They know there's more to the story.

After 9/11 and before Katrina, Mike Brown was a leading champion at FEMA. He warned against redirecting emergency management resources like money and people exclusively toward terrorist events. He argued in favor of a balanced, all-hazards approach.

As the newly-formed Department of Homeland Security began siphoning off FEMA staff for use elsewhere, Brown fought back. He challenged the DHS and the White House when they expressed confidence in the nation's capability to deal with hurricanes based on 9/11 and the Big Four '04 hurricanes in Florida. I recalled that Brown argued that those responses were more a testament to state and local leadership than federal capability, warning that other states had nowhere near the experience and resources of a New York or Florida.

Many changes to FEMA occurred after Katrina, including solidifying the agency's status as a distinct agency within DHS and designating the FEMA administrator as the president's principal advisor for emergency management and disaster response. I believe Brown made similar institutional recommendations before Katrina.

Now, Brown made mistakes at the outset of Katrina, and he gave his side of the story in a 2015 column he wrote for Politico magazine. Yet, does he deserve all the blame? Of course not. Maybe it's worth paying more attention to the battles Brown fought than his nickname. If you want to practice drawing your conclusions, consider Brownie.

RULES AND TOOLS

Following 9/11, the federal government developed the National Incident Management System, commonly known as NIMS, to standardize responses to disasters. After the rollout, I visited a local staging area during a hurricane response. Two staff members were arguing about the new policy.

"You can't do that," one said. "That's not NIMS-compliant."

"Yes, it is," said the other. "What *you're* trying to do—*that's* not NIMS-compliant."

A few minutes later, another responder pulled me aside in confidence. "You know those two guys? Neither one is NIMS-compliant."

One thing that often frustrates independent-thinking emergency managers is when responders turn tools into rules.

After Fugate took over FEMA in 2009, the federal government turned away from issuing plans and strict marching orders, such as national response plans—which had been the formula for decades. Instead, they now publish response and recovery *frameworks* and operational *guidance*.

The philosophy behind this approach is the same one we've been discussing. No disaster unfolds according to the plan. Responders need to be nimble during a crisis. They need to adjust. Using a framework allows you to identify the legal construct, intergovernmental responsibilities, operational resources, and doctrine available. You can then apply what's necessary to tackle the disaster as needs emerge.

Despite the effort within emergency management to shift to a more tool-oriented approach, there will always be people who interpret guidance as strict rules. They want a clear "how-to" for the disaster, even when their instincts and common sense scream: be flexible.

In the 2000 movie *Meet the Parents*, Greg Focker (played by Ben Stiller) stands at the departure gate for his flight home after a disastrous weekend with his fiancée's family. He's waiting alone in the nearly empty terminal. As the flight attendant announces they're ready to begin boarding, Stiller steps up and hands her his ticket.

"I'm sorry, sir," she says, "We're only boarding passengers in rows nine and above at this time."

Stiller looks around. He's the only passenger waiting to board. "I'm in row eight," he says.

"Please step aside, sir."

Stiller dutifully takes half a step to his right. The flight attendant pauses for what appears to be the recommended amount of time in her job manual. Finally, she announces over the loudspeaker that all remaining passengers are now welcome to board.

During your career, you'll ask yourself many times, "Now wait, is that a rule or a tool?" Within the broad scope of operational frameworks lies a reservoir of creative options, potential governmental and nongovernmental partnerships, and ways to deconflict duplicate efforts or leverage programs. It all works as long as you view tools as tools instead of reasons to constrict your options.

PROMOTE THE DOG SITTER

Dwight D. Eisenhower said, "I have always found that plans are useless, but planning is indispensable." The goal of exercises is to test plans, not validate them. Do not be so rigid in your approach that you ignore new ideas and cling to old ones.

The federal urban search and rescue teams never considered that we might need a full-time "search dog media specialist" for a 9/11-type event. It was never in the plan. They did, however, have a public affairs team taught to be innovative and adjust to emerging opportunities.

Inside the Jacob Javits Center, a paper plate overflowed with notes of calls from reporters in the makeshift search-and-rescue media information center. Most of them were about the dogs searching for survivors. An estimated three hundred dogs participated in the response at Ground Zero, the largest deployment of rescue dogs in US history, according to the 9/11 Memorial Museum and the American Kennel Club.

The media and the public had fallen in love with the canine members of FEMA's National Urban Search and Rescue Task Forces. The federal public affairs team supporting the task forces had received more requests about the dogs than any other topic.

This interest created a problem. Too many people were trying to line up interviews with the dog handlers and photo shoots with the dogs. The canine teams were there to search for survivors at Ground Zero, which limited the time they were available for reporters. We struggled to stay in tune with their schedules. It was hard to keep track of which dog teams were rotating off The Pile, who was departing home, and who was coming in.

As the dogs grew more popular, people wanted details about

their names, breeds, training, and recruitment and certification process. Since everyone in our media center handled these calls, everyone had some information, but no one ever had all the information, so we were constantly running back and forth to the dog handlers to ask follow-up questions.

The obvious solution was to give all the dog requests to one person, who would become the subject matter expert. Nothing in the response rule book said we could have a dedicated dog expert, but nothing in it said we couldn't, either. We simply hadn't anticipated this need. Yet the planning process gave us the confidence to adjust within our area of expertise.

The next question was: who should it be?

One day, federal Joint Information Center (JIC) lead Brett Hansard walked by Doug Welty, another search-and-rescue media information team member who had just arrived.

"No, no, no," Doug was saying on the phone. "Not one car. Two cars. I can't put both dogs and their handlers in one car. If you want two canine units on your show, send two cars."

Brett asked him, "Who are you talking to?"

"Larry King at *CNN*."

Brett thought to himself, "We found our guy."

The public affairs crew who worked at the Jacob Javits Center during 9/11 eventually began calling this assignment decision "promoting the dog sitter."

I last spoke with Doug in 2018, three years before he passed away in the fall of 2021. At the time, he was Public Affairs Director at the US Department of State's Office of Inspector General, the latest in a series of high-ranking government jobs he held after 9/11.

Doug grew up in the suburbs of St. Louis and was the grandson of a veterinarian. "Everyone in my neighborhood had pets," he recalled. "Mostly dogs."

Once he was assigned to the search dogs at 9/11, Doug made sure all media requests regarding dogs came to him. He learned every aspect of the canine search mission, established protocols, never turned off his phone, and barely seemed to sleep.

"There were all types of trained dogs," he said. "Some of the crevices were so tight that the bigger dogs, like Bretagne (a golden retriever and member of Texas Task Force 1), could not squeeze through," Doug said. "That's where the Rat Terrier [Ricky from the Puget Sound Task Force] came in handy."

Doug knew every dog and their handlers on a first-name basis. He knew their schedules. He understood the stress the dogs experienced when they couldn't find survivors, and how their handlers needed time to keep the dogs motivated by simulating successful rescues. "The dogs were obsessive. During their breaks from the search, they would chase a toy all day long for a treat. So intense about the job."

More importantly, Doug understood their role in the national urban search-and-rescue system.

"My job was to handle media for the dogs," he said. "Dogs were my specialty, but I did not separate them out. They were as important as any other component of the team—the medical specialist, the firefighters, the structural engineers. Not more important or less important. The dogs were part of the team. I promoted the whole team."

Doug could recite more than the dogs' names. He knew their backgrounds and breeds. When we talked in 2018, he told me about one of his first days working 9/11. "I traveled in a National Guard Humvee, heading down West Side Highway to meet a media pool," he recalled. "It was my third day at 9/11. We had an Australian Shepard in the vehicle. My God, I thought, these dogs are so important to the rescue effort. This dog is all business."

More than anything, Doug said he admired their focus. "When celebrities started showing up at the Javits Center it was a huge morale boost, but some of the search teams got a little starstruck."

The New York Yankees Baseball Team, Susan Sarandon, the guys from Full Metal Jacket, Kyra Sedgwick, Lance Armstrong, Joshua Jackson from Dawson's Creek, and the cast from *The Sopranos* showed up at the Javits Center to meet the search teams. Human rights advocate Bianca Jagger (and the former spouse of Rolling Stones singer Mick Jagger) came by. She quietly said "thank you" over and over again to everyone she met.

Brett remembers the comedian Chevy Chase getting mobbed while the head of the United Nations Commission for Human Rights (the former president of Ireland Mary Robinson) walked through unnoticed. Everyone wanted to meet Derek Jeter, even the Massachusetts USAR Task Force.

"The dogs couldn't care less," Doug remembered. "The search crews dressed some of the Hollywood stars in rescue gear and snuck them to The Pile. All the dogs cared about was the mission. Almost like they were emulating the federal search lead, Pete Bakersky, who was like that too."

As teams rotated in and out of New York, Doug met the new units and stayed connected with the departing ones. He lined up television appearances, magazine profiles, photo documentation projects, and community support events.

"When the federal teams went home," he said, "They asked [Brett's public affairs crew] to help them run an ad in *The New York Times*, thanking the people of New York. The teams were pooling their money to buy the ad. I called *The Times* and asked, 'How much?' *The Times* called back and said, 'How about free?' They ran a full-page ad. We designed it. It had pictures of the teams and the dogs. The teams wanted to thank the people of New York for their support."

Doug helped introduce the world to the search dogs, their handlers, and response teams working the rubble at the World Trade Center, but he had a strict policy.

"We worked only with media who wanted to tell the story of the dogs as part of the teams doing incredible search work," Doug explained. "A TV crew from Japan cared only about the dogs getting massages after they came back from The Pile. I cut them off, but when Oprah [Winfrey] came to do a show, she focused on the dogs' job, how this was a people operation first. The dogs—they were there to help people."

Though the FEMA canine units rescued no survivors during 9/11, the dogs helped recover the remains of firefighters and many other victims. They inspired responders. They captured people's hearts around the globe during an event that was incomprehensible and terrifying. They provided emotional support.

"The search and rescue dogs didn't rescue any people from The Pile," Alan Fausel, executive director of the American Kennel Club's Museum of the Dog, told *The New York Times* on August 30, 2021. "But I think they somewhat rescued the people who were searching."

When you make a decision on a disaster, you never know how it might turn out. Doug turned out to be the right person at the right time for this unique assignment during a moment of history. Some people might say we got lucky.

Yes, responders who adapt and have a foundation of crisis principles often get "lucky." They also have a way of creating positive momentum that carries over to future events. Never underestimate your ability to make a far-reaching contribution during a disaster deployment. The next Doug Welty could be you.

Doug's (and Brett's team's) efforts to tell just one piece of the 9/11 response story led to more community backing once the FEMA teams returned home, solidifying their reputation as local and national resources.

Donations poured in to search dog foundations. The American Kennel Club credited public interest in the 9/11 dogs with advancing the use of therapy dogs at schools, hospitals, and nursing homes.

Since 9/11, FEMA's twenty-eight Urban Search and Rescue Task Forces, with their community-based team members and canine units, have helped save thousands of lives. They have responded to events such as Hurricane Katrina, the 2010 Haiti earthquake, the 2013 Colorado Floods, 2017's Hurricane Harvey, and countless other tragedies.

All of this happened after we promoted the dog sitter.

CHAPTER 6

Be Willing

HOW TO INFLUENCE SUCCESS

"The moment you doubt whether you can fly, you cease forever to be able to do it."

—PETER PAN

A series of tornadoes in 1999 devastated Oklahoma homes and businesses. Photo by Andrea Booher/FEMA.

Former FEMA director James Lee Witt wasn't smiling. We saw him walking through the Baton Rouge Joint Field Office, which was the primary command hub for the statewide Hurricane Katrina response. He had arrived in Louisiana to advise Governor Blanco.

Witt left FEMA four-and-a-half years earlier, in January 2001, during the Clinton-to-Bush administration change. As agency director from 1993–2001, he led the federal response during 350 disasters. He remained involved in emergency management after his FEMA tenure through his consulting firm (as of 2022, named Witt Global Partners).

Considered one of the world's most accomplished emergency managers, he still showed up in most big disasters.

Witt rebuilt, reorganized, and reenergized the agency in the 1990s and dedicated eight years of his life serving as its director. Now, the agency had hit a new low.

Some people weave through a conversation like flowing water. Witt cuts right to the point. "It was a hurricane," he said. "Seven days to prepare. No one had to die."

That was what I believed fueled his grim look that day. He watched as local, state, and federal agencies failed to coordinate. He couldn't believe that the state's citizens were unable to evacuate—and that the government had been unable to help them. He saw leaders who had not led.

Would Witt have made a difference if he had been in the government during Katrina? Definitely, I believe. He was good at his job. More than that, he would have brought the one thing that the Katrina-era leadership needed most of all: more will.

EMERGENCY MANAGER WILL

In emergency management, "will" is the ability to influence a successful disaster recovery because you:

- have a powerful vision for a positive outcome;
- possess the inner strength to stick with your vision; and
- mobilize this power and send it into the disaster.

The first part requires some imagination. The second part needs perseverance. The third part comes free.

Will goes beyond passion and dedication, which is already a job requirement for emergency managers. Think of will as another operational resource, like fire trucks. The difference is that you don't need to refurbish it, requisition it, or buy it.

One emergency manager described the sensation of "will" to me this way:

"Have you ever had a time in emergency management, big or small, when you've felt like you were created for that moment? When you saw a clear path for accomplishing a mission? When you said either to yourself or out loud, 'I want this one?' It can be a rare occurrence. But when it happens, you feel weirdly empowered. You just know you'll get the mission done. That's will."

MY WILL MOMENT

I arrived in Grand Forks, ND in April 1997, right after the levees failed and the mayor ordered the city evacuated. My assignment was to establish a Joint Information Center (JIC) in an annex building at the University of North Dakota.

While setting up the JIC—a large white FEMA communications truck brought up from Denton, Texas after flood waters destroyed city hall—I spent a lot of time in the temporary command trailer for the city and the mayor.

I felt an immediate kinship with the community. A flood had ruined their city. Floodwaters invaded all but the community's western edge. A subsequent fire had damaged or destroyed eleven historic buildings in the downtown core and sixty apartments. They would need years to rebuild to a sustainable level, and about a decade to fully recover.

Yet despite the magnitude of the disaster, the community and local leadership maintained their commitment, energy, and focus. I was overwhelmed with a desire to be a part of their recovery team. I believed something special would happen in Grand Forks, and I wanted in.

One day, outside the city's command trailer, I called Lesli Rucker. The President had appointed her to oversee the federal response to the flooding in North Dakota, which extended beyond Grand Forks. Every county in the state had been declared a disaster area.

"I want something big on this one," I told her. "I don't want just to do PIO. I want to work in Grand Forks, and I'll commit long term."

She was a little taken aback by my passion. Yet she had been in the business for a while. I'm sure she recognized the resolve in my voice.

"Well," Lesli said, "We're opening a satellite disaster field office in Grand Forks. We need a manager who will be our lead federal representative in the city. Do you want it?"

"I'll take it," I said without hesitation. Not even a "What the hell did I just do?" crossed my mind. I felt exhilarated and completely confident I could do the job.

It was a "will" moment.

If you stay in emergency management long enough, you'll have a will moment too. Everyone does.

YOU CAN "WILL" CRISIS SUCCESS OR FAILURE

In a country as rich as the United States, disaster relief rarely fails because of a lack of money. Resources matter, but without grit, determination, and purpose, you are just throwing things at the problem in the hope that something sticks.

Most big disasters teeter on the edge of collapsing into a Katrina-style event. Only the force of individual will brings the event into a manageable fold.

FARGO FLOOD FIGHT 2009

The decision to evacuate is one of the most challenging in emergency management. Often, it's a "damned if you do, damned if you don't" situation. Hurricanes can turn away from the coast. Floodwaters can subside outside city limits, and wildfires can peter out once the winds die down. People rush out from their jobs and regular lives, spend money on gas, food, and hotels—or crash at Aunt Miriam's condo—then return to a clean city and undamaged homes.

The challenge of organizing an evacuation from a large population area is also immense. How long do you wait? What triggers do you use to make the call? You've seen the traffic lines, the runs on food and gas, and the frantic movement of medical patients. Schools close. Businesses shut their doors and lose revenue. Public money gets spent on overtime, contracting resources, and stockpiling supplies. To the dismay of some, even football games get canceled.

Whenever an evacuation occurs and nothing happens, you'll hear tons of grumbling. The opposite, of course, is worse: when communities didn't evacuate and should have. Since Katrina, state and local officials have become much more aggressive in urging evacuations. I've heard more than one sheriff ordering people to evacuate before a hurricane, flood, or wildfire, saying, "If you don't go, leave me info on your next of kin so I'll know who to call when we find your body."

Public safety is ultimately a state and local responsibility, and the call to evacuate belongs to them. Yet the federal government has a role in the process too. That role might include pre-incident training, supplemental planning help, and, in an evacuation, transportation resources or sheltering assistance. It also extends to advice, guidance, and the courage to offer those even when not asked.

All of these elements of an evacuation scenario unfolded in Fargo, North Dakota in 2009.

The Red River Valley in eastern North Dakota is pancake-flat. Prairies and grassland sprinkled with farms, homesteads, and small rural communities dominate the landscape. The largest city in the area, and the state, is Fargo. Population: approximately one hundred thousand as of 2009. North Dakotans joke that their state tree is the telephone pole. The water spreads across roads and highways stretching for miles when it floods.

Fargo sits on the western banks of the Red River of the North. "The Red," as it's often called, is a geographic anomaly that can be confusing to out-of-state flood responders. The river flows north, unlike most US rivers. Therefore, "upstream" is down south and "downstream" is up north. The Red's headwaters form at the confluence of the Bois de Sioux River and the Otter Tail River on the border of Breckenridge, MN and Wahpeton, ND. Its journey ends in Lake Winnipeg in Canada. The largest US city along the Red's 550-mile path is Fargo.

A Cass County, North Dakota home surrounded by flood waters in the spring of 2009. Photo by Michael Rieger/FEMA.

In March 2009, after a winter of heavy snow, the melt began. Eastern North Dakota was already in a fifteen-year wet cycle and had received presidential disaster declarations every year since 1993. After years of floods, the ground remained saturated and the water table full. There was nowhere for the melting snow to go but across the land and into the Red.

As the Red rose, schools emptied. Students from middle-school-age and older joined hockey players, football players, baseball players, teachers, parents, and National Guard soldiers on the lines placing sandbags. City engineers and the US Army Corps of Engineers rushed to construct nearly 80 miles of emergency flood protection including clay and sandbag dikes and a system of linked, dirt and gravel-filled baskets that served as flood barriers.

At the Fargodome, "Sandbag Central" operated around the clock with teams of volunteers. For dirt, the city tore up golf courses, parks, and back yards. Local officials hoped to fill two million sandbags. The community ended up producing six million.

Yet, the water kept rising. By March 25, the prairies, farmlands, parks, and fields north and south of Fargo had gone underwater. The city itself was still dry, hanging on by miles of emergency levees. Based on my experience working the Grand Forks Flood in 1997, FEMA sent me to Fargo to serve as the federal liaison with the city's crisis team. Upon arriving, I checked in with the leadership at the joint Fargo/Cass County Emergency Operations Center and embedded myself at city hall.

Aerial view of Fargo from above the Red River of the North during the 2009 flood fight. Photo by Michael Rieger/FEMA.

The city's command staff conducted meetings morning and night. They received reports nonstop on vulnerable areas throughout the city needing reinforcement. Their catchphrase was "Button Up." They had to button up this neighborhood or button up protection around this service facility. In a March 27 interview with National Public Radio (NPR), Fargo Mayor Dennis Walaker told reporter Peter Schaper, "None of us, no matter how old, has seen the river at these heights. This is uncharted territory."

Meanwhile, state and federal officials watched the rising water with growing alarm. Their biggest worry was, "What's the city's evacuation plan?"

To understand the passion on both sides, you need to remember when this was happening. Spring of 2009 was about three-and-a-half years after Katrina. The last thing the federal government wanted was another disaster of overtopped levees, stranded families, frantic calls for evacuation, and the need to deploy helicopters to rescue survivors off rooftops.

Some of our most horrific and costly disasters in the nation's history occurred when levees or dams failed: Johnstown, PA in 1889; Los Angeles in 1928; Rapid City, SD in 1972; Grand Forks in 1997; and Katrina in 2005. No one wanted to add Fargo to that list.

Nancy Ward, then the acting administrator of FEMA, had already deployed US Fish and Wildlife boat teams to rescue people from isolated farmsteads south of the city. She had marshaled additional relief resources at Grand Forks Air Force Base, located one hundred miles north; deployed a US Coast Guard team; and contracted for 100 ambulances.

As the situation worsened in the final week of March, Ward flew into Fargo for a face-to-face meeting with Walaker. At city hall, she met with the mayor. She was joined by members of North Dakota's congressional delegation and their staff, as well as Governor Hoeven, General Walsh (Commander of the US Army Corps of Engineers Mississippi Valley Division), and other state and federal officials. The group sat at a long, oval-shaped conference table with Walaker at the head and the federal and state officials lining both sides. To Walaker, it must have felt like a full court press.

L-R Congressman Earl Pomeroy, Fargo Mayor Dennis Walaker, Senator Kent Conrad, and FEMA Acting Administrator Nancy Ward during the 2009 Fargo Flood Fight. Photo by Michael Rieger/FEMA.

As the meeting began, the group first talked about the latest flood outlook and ongoing preparations. The federal officials asked about the weather, which is always unpredictable in North Dakota. Bad weather would delay any response, slow supply trucks, and ground rescue helicopters. Finally, Ward asked Walaker what he planned to do next. "It's your call, Mayor," she said. "But let's talk about evacuations—"

"This is not Katrina," said Walaker, cutting her off with a fist slam to the table. "We're not ordering a full evacuation. Some people do need to get out, of course (and thousands did). But we're not issuing a mandatory evacuation for the entire city."

"We're not abandoning the fight," he went on to say. "And we're not ordering our civilian dike watchers and the citizen sandbag crews to stop. We need them. We can still win this one. If we're going down, we're going down swinging."

As the Fargo meeting ended, Walaker held firm. Ward made sure he understood the consequences of his decision and did not have unrealistic expectations about how fast help would arrive.

That evening, I received a late-night call from Meritcare Hospital, the city's largest medical facility. "We think we should evacuate. We need to bounce this off someone. We know it's our decision, but can you talk with us?"

"Look," I said. "I don't know if you're going to win or lose this flood fight. The Army Corps of Engineers is doing a hell of a job, and I trust your local leadership. They know what they're doing. But if you decide to evacuate, you need to make the decision soon, while you can do it as orderly, safely, and comfortably as possible for your patients. It's going to be tough on them."

I was honest about the stakes. "If you wait too long and it floods, it will be difficult," I told the person who had called me. "And those you can't Medivac, you will need to care for while water surrounds you. If you stay, make sure your nurses and doctors can stay, too, and that you've done all you can to protect your facility. Ensure you have emergency power sources, enough food and water, and medical supplies to last for several days, at least. If your staff's under the assumption the state or National Guard or federal government will be able to swoop in the day after the flood, they're wrong. That's not going to happen."

They evacuated.

I saw the person who'd called me the next day at the mayor's daily briefing. "That was a tough decision," I said. "Whichever way you went, I would have been proud of you."

"Thanks," she said, "but the mayor's not happy."

In the end, Meritcare's evacuation proved unnecessary. The hospital rode out the flood unscathed. Again, it's the paradox of evacuation decisions. As Eleanor Roosevelt famously said, "Do what you feel in your heart to be right, for you'll be criticized anyway. You'll be damned if you do and damned if you don't."

Those second-guessing Meritcare's decision may want to look at what happened to New York University Langone Medical Center in Manhattan following Superstorm Sandy in 2012. There, the opposite scenario played out. The medical center didn't evacuate before Sandy struck. Then, stormwater inundated the city's electrical grid, knocked out the facility's power, and "plunged lower Manhattan into darkness," according to an NPR account. The East River surged into the medical complex. The hospital's backup generators didn't work. Suddenly, Langone Medical Center had limited capability to care for patients. They spent all night evacuating three hundred intensive care unit patients to other hospitals, according to an NYU spokeswoman.

I never spoke with Walaker about the Meritcare decision before he died in 2014, so I don't know why he was upset. Maybe he had concerns about the timing of their decision, whether it was premature, and its impact on patients and the city's medical services. Perhaps he also wondered whether the hospital thought he wouldn't let them know in time. That he wouldn't be able to admit defeat, he wouldn't be able to say, "We lost the flood fight." Anyone who ever met Walaker knew that wasn't the case. He was a fighter—but he was a realist, too.

I believe it wasn't Mayor Walaker's ego that caused the frustration. More likely, it reflected his fighting spirit and his will. Exceptional crisis leaders bury their egos but trust their will. Walaker trusted his. I'm sure he wanted others to trust it, too. It was based on years of experience and an intricate knowledge of the Red River, its tributaries, the city's capabilities, and how to fight a Fargo flood.

The sixty-eight-year-old mayor had lived his entire life in the community. In February, before the melt began, he would spend early mornings south of the city, trampling through snow drifts to measure the snowpack in the fields and study the water levels on the Wild Rice River, which feeds into the Red.

Before he was mayor, Walaker was Fargo's Director of Public Works. And before that, he had overseen the city's emergency management, forestry, and fleet management operations. He had designed, built, tested, and exercised nearly all the city's flood-fighting infrastructure and built a loyal team of like-minded public servants. He had fought and won every flood fight over the past thirty years.

Walaker knew flood fighting. He also knew the Red River could beat him. He expected someday it would, and he always said that unless Fargo received funding to build permanent flood protection—like Grand Forks and New Orleans—they would one day lose the city.

But that wasn't the case in 2009. Though it would be close, Fargo got the little bit of luck it needed. A few days before the crest arrived, the weather turned. It got cold, with temperatures dropping to seven degrees by the time the Red crested on March 28, earlier than expected. Rain turned into snow, water froze, the melt slowed, and the peak leveled and passed the city. In some parts of Fargo, the Red came within "inches of overtopping the dikes," *The Fargo Forum* newspaper reported. The final crest reached 40.84 feet, the highest level ever recorded in the community. There was still nearly $100 million in damages, but it wasn't catastrophic.

The federal government was responsible for letting Walaker know the consequences if he didn't evacuate and lost the fight. And he had the responsibility as the city's leader to make the final decision in his community's best interest. In the end, he was right. By engaging him to defend his decision, so was Nancy Ward. Both displayed leadership. Both displayed will.

WILLING CRISIS FAILURE

The danger of will is that it can work both ways. Just as you can "will" success, you can also "will" failure.

In a crisis, your attitude and words matter. What you say and how you say it conveys what you believe. Your words and tone tell your team whether you expect to succeed or fail.

I worked with a federal official whose job was to help prepare the nation to respond to a catastrophic earthquake. During team briefings, he would joke, "After the earthquake hits, I'll be fired. The country will need someone to blame. It will be me. I've told my family to 'be prepared for negative headlines about your dad.'"

I'm sure this sounded clever and astute among his political friends. He knew how the political world worked and loved to talk about it. I thought it sounded disappointingly defeatist. Worse, he would say it to his team and employees, the very people who would be responding and that he would be leading. He predicted failure before the disaster happened, when there still might be years to prepare.

I asked our top military liaison, a colonel who served in Iraq and Afghanistan, if officers tell their troops, "Well, we're probably going to lose the war, but I guess we should go fight regardless."

"Right," he said sarcastically.

As part of the congressional investigation post-Katrina, several internal correspondences among response leaders leaked out. Among the chatter, some memos read along the lines, "I have a bad feeling about this hurricane," and "I'm not confident we can handle this one."

Defeat is a self-fulfilling prophecy. Say you will fail before the crisis starts, and there is no chance you will succeed. Coming from a leader, that negative attitude permeates the organization. Failure is expected. Then when it happens, everyone says, "See, I told you so."

It's bad enough when a single leader starts willing defeat. It's worse when an entire chorus of leaders join in.

In 2007 at an international conference, a reporter from the New Orleans *Times-Picayune* appeared. His subject was Katrina. As he gave his presentation, he grew angrier and angrier. His face turned red, and his eyes watered as he delivered a powerful, emotional summary of the recovery. It was all negative: the still-wrecked buildings, the piles of debris, and thousands of families without a permanent home.

This reporter struck me as someone who cared deeply for his city, and his presentation reflected the frustration still prevalent in southeast Louisiana nearly two years after the hurricane. He was reporting what he heard and saw. His message, to sum it up, was, "No one cares about us. Nothing's getting done. There is no hope."

He was not the only one with this impression. It became a common refrain among Louisiana leadership, many national leaders, and the media. And it turned into a self-fulfilling prophecy. The more survivors heard that nothing was being accomplished, the more faith they lost in government, and the more the recovery stalled. What he said was true, but it didn't have to be.

The origins of the "no help, no hope" message came early in the disaster, when the levees broke. The purpose was to ignite support, raise the alarm, and kick-start an otherwise tragically slow response, which was compounded by a failure to evacuate the area prior to the storm.

While the Katrina response was proceeding well in Mississippi, thanks to a stronger federal, state, and local crisis leadership team, Louisiana's situation was getting worse. The hurricane affected both states tremendously—Louisiana with the flooding, and Mississippi with the winds and storm surge.

The helplessness even infected me. During a low moment, I

talked to my former boss, Morrie Goodman, who arrived at Katrina as part of James Lee Witt's advisory team. "I don't know, Morrie," I told him. "Maybe FEMA can't handle disaster response. Maybe Congress needs to change the law and give that responsibility to the Coast Guard. In the future, we'll just do recovery."

Morrie stared at me. "What? Are you crazy? Coordinating the federal response is FEMA's job. There is no one else. Of course you can do it."

Eventually, the life-threatening situation in Louisiana stabilized. Coast Guard Admiral Thad Allen, who replaced FEMA's Mike Brown as the Principal Federal Official for the disaster, provided order at the federal level. People stopped dying. The rescues ended, and the Army Corps of Engineers pumped out the floodwater, sending the overflow to the Gulf of Mexico. By the end of 2005, it seemed the recovery had the potential to gain some momentum. Yet it turned out the anger, frustration, and helplessness of the early days would be hard to overcome.

Big disasters are complex, and floods cause the worst destruction among natural disasters. They trap people inside homes, invade hospitals, wreak havoc on public safety facilities, and inundate all the below-ground infrastructure that makes a community livable. It can be hard to recognize progress when facing so much devastation. That's why a demonstration of leadership "will" is so essential to disaster recovery.

After the 1994 Northridge Earthquake in California, a survivor told me, "You have to know what it means when you have lost everything after a disaster, to see federal responders and out-of-state volunteers in your community. You will hear a lot of negative things, but there's something powerful and uplifting when you realize your nation, your country, knows what has happened to you and has come to help." That insight stayed with me.

Unlike the early years in New Orleans, the leadership supporting Grand Forks made it a point to celebrate recovery milestones, no matter how small, following their 1997 flood. Every time Lesli Rucker or James Lee Witt came to check on the community, they would point out the progress. One day, there would be tons of discarded flood-damaged belongings piled ten feet high outside homes and buildings; a year later, much of the debris would be gone. The houses in some neighborhoods would appear repaired and repainted, the grass greener, and newly-planted flowers bloomed in several gardens. Nearby, a school would have reopened. Lesli and James Lee would point those out and say, "Yes, you still have a long way to go, but look how far you've already come." City officials would hold onto those words and share them with the community to encourage residents.

"You don't know how much that meant to us," former Grand Forks City Council President Hal Gershman told me. "When you live with the disaster every day, month after month, year after year, and it's all you talk about, it's hard to see you're accomplishing something. Thank you for telling us."

During Hurricane Katrina, the US Coast Guard rescued 33,500 people. In addition, 1,777 FEMA Urban Search and Rescue team members and their dogs saved or assisted another 6,582 survivors from the floodwaters and recovered more than 300 human remains. Federal helicopter pilots, rescue swimmers, firefighters, doctors, and nurses from the states of Texas, Colorado, New York, Nebraska, Massachusetts, Florida, and California showed up and saved tens of thousands of lives.

The Southeast Louisiana Task Force, composed of local fire and law enforcement personnel, spent two months conducting a final search for remains in New Orleans' Lower Ninth Ward before debris-removal operations began. They hoped to ensure that no victim was left behind. Hundreds of thousands of volunteers arrived from relief organizations like the American Red Cross, Salvation Army, Humane Society, United Way, Direct Relief, and Catholic Charities. They fed people, helped repair homes, gave supplies, and picked up debris for free.

At the neighborhood level, thousands of southeast Louisiana families rebuilt their homes while damaged businesses reopened and people created new ones. Community-based organizations emerged and filled the governmental leadership void, laying partnership foundations that would pay big dividends in the years ahead. People like the public affairs team at the Governor's Office of Homeland Security and Emergency Preparedness (GOHSEP) and FEMA's Robert Josephson and Gail Adams worked tirelessly to build and sustain intergovernmental relationships. Presidential Medal of Freedom recipient and President of Xavier University, Norman C. Francis, Ph.D, reopened the school in January 2006 with "75 percent of the pre-Katrina student body, a feat many doubted was possible," *New Orleans Magazine* noted in 2015.

Yet you hardly heard anything positive emanating from Louisiana in the first few years after Katrina. It seemed the negative stories drowned out the positive effort. You can always find examples of success, even in the aftermath of a disaster like Katrina, but they can feel invisible when leadership tells everyone that nothing has improved.

Sixteen months after Katrina struck, former senator John Edwards kicked off his candidacy for president, with the devastation of New Orleans as his backdrop. Edwards announced his bid "framed by two ruined homes and a dead tree," reported *The New York Times*. For years, vendors in the French Quarter sold t-shirts that read: "Where's FEMA?! Federal Employees Missing Again," and "FEMA Evacuation Plan: Run, Motherfucker, Run."

Experienced federal, state, and local recovery workers below the political level tested ideas and advanced experimental initiatives to address issues. Yet they often found their efforts ridiculed by other organizations and in the media when their programs didn't solve problems immediately. Every federal blunder, even the more inconsequential errors, was highlighted, publicized, and re-publicized by the Louisiana congressional delegation and other members of Congress, as yet another example of federal incompetence.

Survivor trust in the government was eroded. People were given little reason to believe in or cooperate with an emergency management system that appeared broken.

The senior disaster recovery assignment slots in New Orleans seemed to become plug-and-play positions, as if anyone with government leadership experience could handle the complex programmatic duties. It was like assuming a popular political operative was qualified to command an aircraft carrier, or a winning college quarterback would make a great goalie for the New York Rangers simply because he was a talented athlete.

It was not until 2009 that the approach changed at the federal level when newly-appointed FEMA Administrator Craig Fugate put Tony Russell in charge of the federal office for Louisiana hurricane recovery. When Russell arrived, it was the first time a professional emergency manager with extensive field experience directing federal disaster recovery programs had headed the office since its inception three years earlier.

When you tell people that no one cares, you're telling them to give up. You may think it's helping you fight for resources and dollars, but most people outside the impacted area will stop paying much attention after a few months. The ones who hear your message the loudest will be your residents.

I deployed to southeast Louisiana in 2005, 2006, and 2008. I never met anyone who didn't care and wasn't trying to help. I worked with a lot of intergovernmental teams where people didn't get along. For years, the federal government fought with the state, the state argued with parishes, and the parishes competed with one another for money, resources, and attention. All this played out in the public arena. The message survivors heard the loudest was: no one cares and nothing is getting done. Cooperation crumbled, projects got delayed, communication stopped, and hope faded. This harmful "will" application delayed recovery in southeast Louisiana for years.

Fortunately, the New Orleans Saints won the Super Bowl in 2010, which changed everything. I'm semi-serious. It was a kick start, a non-political event that many people could get behind. It generated community pride and symbolized the Katrina come-back, sparking renewed interest in the city. The locals took pride in highlighting their struggles and successes—just like their football team.

Dr. Jacqueline McBride-Jones has not only helped communities recover from disasters but has bounced back from personal setbacks. In speaking about Katrina, she told me: "Everyone has an inherent will to survive, to contribute to recovery, to be of service to others—even if it is just within our own families. The key is calling that will to remembrance. Sometimes we forget that."

At the same time as the Saints competed in their Super Bowl season, a new style of recovery leadership was beginning to emerge; one that was less caustic and more focused on consensus- building, leveraging resources, and improving coordination. "New Orleanians went from mourning the loss of our city to rage about what really happened to hope for the future and taking action. It worked," Ruthie Frierson, founder and chair emeritus for Citizens for 1 Greater New Orleans told *New Orleans Magazine* in August 2015. The teams rebuilding southeast Louisiana had enough enemies. It was time to make more friends.

One person who made me a friend, fan, and supporter of Louisiana was Mitch Landrieu. While working Hurricane Gustav in 2008, I attended Governor Jindal's daily Unified Command meetings. After one session, during which I had said and contributed nothing while sitting against the wall with the other backbenchers, Lieutenant Governor Landrieu sought me out, weaving his way through the crowded room.

"Hey, I just want to thank you for all you're doing," he said, extending a hand and a smile to introduce himself.

It was an incredibly kind gesture. I sat nowhere near the top of the response hierarchy. I was a federal spokesperson, so perhaps Landrieu had heard one of my interviews. Maybe he saw my FEMA shirt, appreciated the agency's overall effort, and decided it was "thanking Ed the Fed" day. Whatever the motivation, I've never forgotten that moment. It lifted me, made me want to be on his team, and inspired me to work resolutely for his state.

Fast-forward to 2012, when I'm back in New Orleans for Hurricane Isaac. By then, Landrieu was mayor of the city. His office called for help arranging FEMA presence at an upcoming press conference. I promised to have someone there, then added some unsolicited advice:

"Be inclusive," I said. "I've met your mayor before. He builds recovery partnerships publicly. He encourages coordination and communication among anyone who can lend a hand or dollar to the fight. He's positive. I like it. It reminds me a lot of how New York City did it after 9/11."

They didn't need my advice. The mayor's office knew precisely the tone they wanted. "We've looked at New York's 9/11 crisis management approach," his press person told me. "They did some good things."

WILLING CRISIS SUCCESS

A few years before my conversation with Landrieu's press office—as the mind shift in southeast Louisiana began to take root—St.

Bernard Parish also looked for a new approach to managing its disaster recovery. Almost three years had already passed since Katrina's floodwaters and a resulting oil spill wreaked havoc in the parish. Yet many areas in the community remained in ruins. The new Parish President, Craig Taffaro, needed to ignite the recovery.

A resilience story caught Taffaro's attention. He heard about how Grand Forks, North Dakota, had come back from one of the costliest floods in US history. The community stood rebuilt, more robust, and safer than before as a model for disaster recovery.

The inspiration for connecting the two communities came from FEMA's Barb Sturner. She had worked on both the Grand Forks flood and the Katrina recovery in St. Bernard. Sturner spent years in both communities and saw similarities. Grand Forks had a slightly larger population, but both communities suffered flood disasters that resulted from levee failures. Both sustained devastating impacts to homes, businesses, and infrastructure. And each faced similar challenges managing complex long-term recovery.

Sturner pitched the idea of a St. Bernard field trip. Grand Forks immediately agreed to host the Louisiana visitors. At first, Taffaro questioned whether a community that hadn't experienced a historic hurricane could understand what St. Bernard was going through. Sturner persisted, and Taffaro eventually agreed the visit was worth a shot.

"Our trip was to say, 'Hey, those guys have been doing this for years. Why don't we take a look at what they are doing?'" Taffaro recalled in 2022.

One of the surest signs of forward-leaning crisis leadership is the willingness to ask for management help. St. Bernard Parish did not ask its new sister city for money or resources. What they hoped for was advice, technical assistance, and lessons learned. In June 2008, Taffaro and eight other St. Bernard officials and citizens headed to Grand Forks.

Taffaro and his team spent four days in the city. They met with government department heads and business owners, engineers, and community leaders. They toured mitigation projects. They visited with the city's buoyant mayor, Dr. Michael Brown—who replaced Pat Owens in 2000 and led the community's long-term recovery. And they spent half a day discussing lessons with leaders from East Grand Forks, MN, a community of nine thousand residents across the Red River. The two cross-state northern communities had coordinated throughout the 1997 flood aftermath.

The St. Bernard's delegation spoke with Grand Forks and East Grand Forks representatives whose homes the flood had also damaged. The two groups compared notes on managing a community's recovery while running their own. They spoke to business owners who had rebuilt and shared ideas about restarting economic development. They met survivors.

The Grand Forks hosts explained their decisions, policies, and strategies—both those that worked and those that didn't. They encouraged their visitors to get out, meet the community, see the results, talk to people, and judge for themselves. And when the St. Bernard parish team walked through the neighborhoods, people thanked them.

One of Grand Forks' recovery hallmarks has been outward

appreciation for the help they received. Their flood forced fifty-two thousand residents to flee from their homes. At the time, it was the largest single-city evacuation in the United States since the Civil War, according to the city's official website, grandforksgov.com.

Grand Forks residents ended up in every state, staying with friends or family. They experienced kindness from strangers, local governments, and area volunteers while waiting for the waters to recede at home. Volunteers poured into the disaster area from across the country, including Louisiana.

Grand Forks' leadership spoke about their responsibility to spend federal and state assistance grants wisely and respectfully by building a more robust infrastructure so people wouldn't have to pay again. They felt they owed the country gratitude. They also felt compassionate toward other communities affected by disasters. In the city's view, the St. Bernard trip was another chance to pay back the country, and the city embraced the opportunity to say thank you.

Grand Forks provided their visitors with case studies, data, and concrete examples. They were candid about the most demanding moments: frustration, anger, depression; divorces and sudden heart attacks; resignations and departures; disagreements with FEMA; and how they got through it all. The city's unsinkable mayor Brown shared his "You win, I win" approach to building collaborative partnerships and overcoming chasms between federal, state, and local agencies.

Everywhere the St. Bernard team went, they saw a unified community spirit. A high school ensemble serenaded them outside city hall with songs from a musical written locally by students and teachers in the first summer after the flood, titled Keep the Faith. They heard over and over the community's simple recovery motto: "We said we could, we said we would, and we did."

"The trip to Grand Forks helped us just take a breath," Taffaro said. "There was color. There were sounds. There was joy and life and an active, thriving community. It was good for us to be in that and then overlay the concept that this was a community that was completely devastated.

"It connected the hope," he said.

As you build a network of relationships during your career, you'll have opportunities to introduce people from various communities. There's value in those peer-to-peer connections. Consider it another tool for your emergency management toolkit.

The concept of sharing lessons, offering encouragement, and fostering "will" certainly seems to have taken hold between North Dakota and Louisiana. In 2011, three years after St. Bernard's visit to Grand Forks, the Souris River in north-central North Dakota surged to historic levels. Floodwaters overtopped the levee system protecting the cities of Minot and Burlington. The flood caused massive damage and forced ten thousand people to evacuate. Among the first organizations to reach out to Minot and offer help included the Beacon of Hope, a volunteer group formed in the aftermath of Katrina, and based in New Orleans.

A FINAL THOUGHT ON BUILDING WILL

In the novel *Islands in the Stream*, Ernest Hemingway describes a father and son who are deep-sea fishing in the Caribbean. The son hooks a fish and tries for hours to reel it in. His hands are bleeding, shoulders raw and aching, his throat parched from the salt air and beating sun. Someone on the boat asks if they should help the boy, but the father refuses. "Please know I would have stopped this long ago except that I know that if David catches this fish, he'll have something inside him for all his life, and it will make everything else easier."

I read this book forty years ago, and that passage has stayed with me. When you do something hard, it's inside you forever, and you can draw on it again and again. The more you do difficult things, the more "will" you'll have to accomplish new ones.

CHAPTER 7

Facing Failure

HOW TO OVERCOME PROFESSIONAL SCREWUPS, MISTAKES, AND SETBACKS

"Adversity does, I think, allow a person to grow, to feel more empathy, to feel wisdom, and, more importantly, to feel perspective."

—DORIS KEARNS GOODWIN

Caption: FDNY rescuers, FEMA's Pete Bakersky, and Colorado Lt. Governor Joe Rogers at New York City's Ground Zero during the 9/11 response. Photo by Michael Rieger/FEMA.

When Katrina hit, FEMA sent me to Houston, where I was shocked to find that I was one of the few FEMA staff on the scene. I checked into the Incident Command Post (ICP) at the Houston Reliant Center, which managed relief efforts for the hundreds of thousands of Katrina evacuees who fled to south Texas. The command staff gave me a desk and cardboard name tent labeled "FEMA Liaison."

The ICP was made up of all-stars from the local emergency management community and leadership from city and county offices, including then-Harris County Judge, Robert Eckels.

It was a crushing time for FEMA, the epitome of a quicksand disaster where everything goes wrong—and the more you fight to get out, the deeper you sink. News stories ran twenty-four hours a day, and the criticism of FEMA was universal and non-stop. It was critical to demonstrate a confident, capable, and in-control presence to prevent public trust in the agency from further dissolving.

On my fifth night there, I rushed in late for the Fire Chief's shift change brief and right into the extension cord powering his slide projector. I lurched toward a nearby desk, scattering a doctor's work papers across the floor. The projector teetered at the edge of the table, its light now directed at me. I could sense every one of the 40 people in the room shaking their heads and thinking, "Typical FEMA."

When you work in emergency management, you are guaranteed to experience professional setbacks. Sometimes you'll be the one who screws up. You'll also run into obstacles like a difficult boss or impossible assignments. In my professional capacity,

I've been called an idiot, knucklehead, loser, spinner of the truth, and a flat-out disappointment. Each time, I had to figure out what I did wrong and what to do instead next time around.

Sometimes the screwups occur way above your head, but you'll still need to help deal with the consequences. At different times in its history, the agency I used to work for has been branded as bungling, incompetent, uncaring, or a disaster on top of a disaster. Following Hurricane Hugo in 1989, when I joined FEMA, Senator Ernest Fritz Hollings called us "the sorriest bunch of bureaucratic jackasses [he'd] ever seen." More than once, FEMA has had to remake itself following setbacks.

This chapter is about professional failure. We've all been there, and if you stay in this business long enough, you'll be there again. Yet, emergency managers would take home the gold if comebacks were an Olympic sport. You can recover from any screw-up, no matter how consequential, as long as you believe no failure is permanent.

FAILURES ARE INEVITABLE

At a training I attended long ago, the flip chart read, "When things break, we go to work. We help fix what's broken. That's what emergency managers do." I have never forgotten that.

Being involved in emergency response at any level means you'll often need to make decisions quickly and decisively with limited information. Sometimes those decisions work, and sometimes they won't. Calamities are often precipitated or magnified by avoidable failure. Tragedies have occurred because of risk intelligence, levee, or evacuation failures. Disasters have been made worse or accelerated because of coordination or communication failures. Failure can happen in this business in many ways, which is one of the reasons it's inevitable. Luckily, inevitable does not mean irreversible.

Accepting that failures will occur makes you less likely to be thrown into a tizzy when they do.

YOU'RE NOT IN THE FAILURE BUSINESS. YOU'RE IN THE COMEBACK BUSINESS

During the week of March 12, 2020, the repercussions of COVID-19 came like a tidal wave. Schools and businesses were closed and planes grounded. The whole world was shutting down. I ran into a newly-unemployed friend sitting outside a café, casually sipping his beer.

"You're looking calm," I said.

"I'm thinking about what stocks I'm going to buy," he told me.

"You're not worried about the economic devastation because of COVID-19?"

"It's like this," he said. "It is either the end of the world, or not. I'm betting the world will recover. When it does, I'll win too. And if it is the end of the world, then what does it matter?"

Many years ago, I sought guidance from FEMA's tribal liaison, Scott Logan, during a professional rough patch.

"In emergency management, you can come back from anything," he told me. You, too, should be confident you can handle setbacks.

Whether you have experienced setbacks personally, as a member of an organization, or as a disaster survivor, the ordeal can be harrowing, emotionally wrenching, and difficult to overcome. Yet when you work in emergency management, viewing failure as irreversible is basically giving up.

Responders, survivors, communities, and organizations can come back from even the most devastating and monumental failures. In this line of work, we're reminded of it every day.

Screw-ups can be learning experiences. Setbacks can turn into comebacks. And failures can become transformational gifts if you emerge stronger in the long run. Winston Churchill once said, "Success is not final, failure is not fatal. It is the courage to continue that counts." Former FEMA director James Lee Witt and author James Morgan wrote a book in 2002 emphasizing the same theme: *Stronger in the Broken Places: Nine Lessons for Turning Crisis Into Triumph.*

HOW TO DEAL WITH SETBACKS

Navigating your way out of screw-ups can take time, and the pain of the experience will linger. However, you can't be afraid to fail. Don't join the crisis enablers and the repetitive i-dotters and t-crossers. They talk a lot, they conduct analyses, but they *never* act. If you really want to mess up big-time on a disaster, don't do anything until you've created the perfect plan and found the perfect moment to unveil it. Theodore Roosevelt said, "In any moment of decision, the best thing to do is the right thing, the next best thing to do is the wrong thing, and the worst thing to do is nothing,"

For two reasons, most crisis leaders don't want to work with people who have never failed. First, the experience provides empathy and a necessary perspective for handling a disaster. People who have tasted failure tend to understand what disaster survivors are going through.

Second, you'll find the "Golden Child" often disappears once the crisis hits. That's because they have never failed publicly and may fear it happening on the big stage. If they show up, they typically spend too much time seeking approval from above to cover themselves if things go wrong. You'll always wonder if you can count on them when things get ugly.

Give every crisis assignment your best shot, but realize there will be times you'll miss the mark. What's more important is what you do next. Here are strategies for managing a setback and ways to mitigate the consequences of falling short in the first place:

1. Get your mindset right.
2. Deal with setbacks.
3. Overcome setbacks.

GET YOUR MINDSET RIGHT

Remember when you fail that you're not the first person to do so. As Roman emperor and Stoic philosopher Marcus Aurelius wrote, "Bear in mind, all this happened before. All just the same. Only the people are different."

Here are three ways to develop a frame of mind that will help you deal with setbacks:

1. Show your poise.
2. Embrace the fear of failure.
3. Pack the "Wow" tip.

SHOW YOUR POISE

Crisis leaders watch you most closely after you have made a mistake or experienced a setback. They want to see whether you're brave enough to tackle the situation and if you have what it takes to turn it around.

"Everyone knows you care, and you're disappointed," FEMA's Steve Olsen advised me after one of my missteps. "But remember, people are never watching you more closely than after a disappointment. This is an opportunity to show the organization what type of person you are. Don't blame, shout, or complain. Handle it with grace."

When you screw up, it's easy to lose your cool. That's why it's best to be prepared to respond. How do you want to be perceived? Calm and collected, or angry and defensive? Will the people watching you feel reassured or doubtful of your abilities to deal with the situation? As frustrating as any setback may be, it's also a chance to show people what kind of crisis leader you can be.

EMBRACE THE FEAR

In the 2000 football movie *The Replacements*, the coach, played by Gene Hackman, asks the team to admit their fears.

"I'm scared of spiders, coach," one player says helpfully. Others chime in, "Me too."

"That's not what I'm talking about. I'm talking about what scares us on the football field."

"Bees," says one player.

"Anyone here afraid of anything other than insects?"

"Quicksand," the quarterback offers based on experience. "You're playing, and you think everything is going fine. Then one thing goes wrong. And then another. And another. You try to fight back, but the harder you fight, the deeper you sink. Until you can't move… You can't breathe…because you're in over your head. Like quicksand."

Some of my screw-up experiences felt like that. The message is about overcoming failure and embracing the fears associated with it. Before jumping into the fixing, try admitting there's been a mistake first.

Any comeback needs to start with acknowledging you've fallen short and it has rocked you. Be honest about the mistake and own it. Once you've done that, you'll be positioned to overcome or mitigate the situation. Don't worry about the bees. Focus on navigating the quicksand.

PACK THE "WOW" TIP

This tip might sound goofy, but many industry professionals use it in some form.

When you're in the middle of a messy situation, it's helpful to step back and get perspective. As someone who screwed up a lot, here's a story I heard that I've used to jolt me out of any freeze-up.

One day, four grandchildren went on a road trip with Grandpa. While Grandpa tried to concentrate on driving, the kids in the back seat squirmed, fought, and threw crackers. Finally, Grandpa had enough. He turned around and yelled, "Stop talking and calm down!"

The backseat went still. Except for the youngest one, who stared at Grandpa in admiration and then said, *"Wow!"*

The youngest child was impressed by the impact of Grandpa's explosive voice taking control of the situation. We call this reaction "the wow technique."

Saying "wow" refocuses your attention on being present in the moment and remembering what you are grateful for instead of focusing on the negative. I used the wow technique to remind myself that despite temporary frustrations, it was still a privilege to be part of any emergency response. When you feel overwhelmed or discouraged by your job, boss, or disaster, say "wow."

DEALING WITH SETBACKS

When setbacks happen, it's good to have a standby plan to tackle any screwup. You might not need every part of the plan every time. Just pick and choose what works depending on the situation.

1. Describe your plan.
2. Seek guidance.
3. Consider apologizing.
4. Try being self-deprecating.

DESCRIBE YOUR PLAN

When you screw up, immediately let people know you're taking action to tackle it. If you aren't sure what to say, use the "think in threes" concept. For example:

1. Here's the problem.
2. Here are the specific steps I'm taking.
3. Here's how I hope to mitigate the consequences or ensure this doesn't happen again.

It may seem simple, but often the most reassuring words a crisis leader can say after any setback are, "I have a plan. Here's what we're going to do."

SEEK GUIDANCE

Part of your plan should be to ask for help.

One of the best things about working in emergency management is that people genuinely want you to bounce back. The mission is to help the cause, not rake employees over the coals for every decision. Almost everyone I went to for help after my screwups shared their own setback stories and offered insight. Your coworkers in emergency management are there to give help, so ask for it.

CONSIDER APOLOGIZING

When delivered sincerely and followed by action, the apology is a powerful tool for dealing with stumbles. Following Hurricane Katrina, the US Army Corps of Engineers apologized and acknowledged responsibility for the levee failure. Later, with funding from Congress, the Corps not only fixed the levees but improved flood protection around New Orleans. After the Parkland, Florida school shooting in 2018, the FBI apologized for ignoring tips that should have raised concerns about the shooter and revised internal procedures in response.

Legislators, the public, and higher-ups inevitably demand change after a high-profile failure. Leaders and leaders-in-the-making can either own the mistake and help shape those changes or let them happen outside their control.

In my experience, the best crisis leaders wanted to be part of the process. Often, the opportunity to influence the outcome starts with an apology. It shows you recognize the problem and have the confidence to fix it. As author and culture journalist Steven Ivory once said, "Apologize. Go all-in. Leave no stone unturned. If the apology is sincere, forgiveness will follow."

I once apologized to a journalist from a Montana newspaper who had written articles about disasters. Without her asking, I sent glowing biographies of our leadership along with pictures and a suggestion that she use this material to write about my agency. She was not impressed. The resulting article tore me up and spat me out for wasting her time. I called her and apologized.

"You're right. I'm an emergency information officer, not a publicist," I said. "I need to focus on getting out news people can use in case of disasters instead of bragging about my agency."

The columnist was right. I also think my call surprised her. We ended up having a productive conversation. I hung her column in my office as a reminder.

TRY BEING SELF-DEPRECATING

During the run-up to the 2002 Winter Olympics in Salt Lake City, Utah, my external affairs team supported the state-run Joint Information Center (JIC), located in the basement of Utah's State Capitol Building. One of the biggest stories in the final weeks was the arrival of high-level politicians to assess the preparation. They weren't evaluating the quality of the ice rinks or the snow depth on the ski slopes. They were considering the event's ability to keep people safe.

2002 was no ordinary Olympics. It was the most prominent international event since the 9/11 terrorist attacks. There had been rumors about canceling the games. The country felt vulnerable to another attack, and this event would offer quite a target to evildoers. Ultimately, the US decided to proceed. The federal and state government poured money and resources into the area for security. Media cameras came to highlight the effort, and politicians soon followed.

The politicians enjoyed the beautiful Utah mountains between public safety and security assessments. Time and time again, we'd hear stories of how they, too, could have been winter sports stars if only an injury had not derailed their athletic career. After watching a member of President Bush's cabinet swooshing down the slopes at Park City, a television news reporter speculated that he, too, could have been a champion if it wasn't for a skiing accident that tore up his knee.

Brett Hansard had heard enough. "How come whenever a politician doesn't become a professional athlete, it's always because they got hurt, and it's never because they weren't good enough?" he said aloud to the JIC team.

To build a team that can withstand mistakes, try this:

1. Be self-deprecating.
2. Tell a story about failing because you weren't good enough, what you learned, and how you bounced back.
3. Describe experiences that encourage colleagues to take risks and persevere when things don't work out at first.

Disaster recovery is a long haul. Each one will have accomplishments and setbacks. Inspirational crisis leaders learn to talk about both. Those who share stories that don't feature themselves as heroes often give the best lessons.

OVERCOMING SETBACKS

Here are six ways to help you mitigate, overcome, and even benefit from setbacks:

1. Surround yourself with positive people.
2. Focus on the mission.
3. Choose coordination over control.
4. Be a priority gatekeeper.
5. Don't assume you are failing.

6. Consider feedback a gift.

SURROUND YOURSELF WITH POSITIVE PEOPLE

Before FEMA consolidated hiring for its reserve program at headquarters, I recruited hundreds of people for disaster field jobs with the agency. I never worried about their GPA, experience, tactical skills, or program knowledge. We had training programs for that. I wanted people willing to spend their first year taking on all the jobs that no one else wanted. Someone who believed every position on a disaster contributed to the overall mission and would tackle everything with enthusiasm.

Arkadi Kuhlman, founder and former CEO of ING Direct USA, said in a 2011 interview with the Harvard Business Review, "If you want to renew and reenergize an industry, don't hire from that industry. I'd rather hire a jazz musician, a dancer, or a captain in the Israeli army. They can learn about banking."

A former executive at Southwest Airlines, Sherry Phelps, said she evaluated prospective employees apart from their airline experience. "The first thing we looked for was the warrior spirit."

People with a positive attitude are more willing to embrace something new, spot the exception, promote a bold idea, stick their neck out, and, when they fail, be ready to try again. They are irrepressible in the face of setbacks and generally happy and fun to be around. If you want to improve your (and your organization's) ability to stay out of quicksand, it pays to surround yourself with positive people.

FOCUS ON THE MISSION

Don't make the mission about you.

In Chapter 2, we talked about burying your ego. It's a great way to help you step up on any disaster assignment. If you ranked why specific disaster responses fail, big egos would be high, if not first, on that list. Take the 1900 Galveston Hurricane. According to History Magazine, even more than 120 years later, it "remains the deadliest natural disaster in American History." Historians estimate the death toll may have reached twelve thousand people. Unchecked egos deserve much of the blame.

American weathercaster and journalist Al Roker explains this in his book, *The Storm of the Century: Tragedy, Heroism, Survival, and the Epic True Story of America's Deadliest Disaster: The Great Gulf Hurricane of 1900.*

In 1900, Willis Moore was the director of the United States Weather Bureau, the predecessor to the National Weather Service. He envied advancements Cuba had made in weather forecasting. Rather than build a partnership with Cuba to exchange information and coordinate efforts, he had the Bureau cut off communications between them.

Under Moore's direction, the Weather Bureau centralized the control of weather information by limiting the ability of their local forecasters to issue weather outlooks. He didn't trust his field experts, believing they would exaggerate weather threats and cause the public to panic.

These two ego-driven decisions proved fatal in 1900. As a hurricane roared north of Cuba and entered the Gulf of Mexico, the Bureau's national office guessed wrong. Moore called the weather system "not a hurricane" and predicted the storm would curve toward Florida.

On September 8, 1900, the category four hurricane slammed into Galveston. As the storm arrived, the Weather Bureau's overconfident Galveston forecaster, Isaac Cline, realized the magnitude of his agency's error.

Without waiting for Moore's approval, he defied the ban on local weather warnings and desperately issued an official hurricane alert. He was too late. Rising seawater had destroyed bridges to the mainland, cutting off evacuation routes. Low-lying Galveston offered few places of refuge. The ocean surge swept away homes, buildings, and people. The thousands who died in the storm waters included Cline's pregnant wife.

A dose of humility, vulnerability, and good listening skills go a long way in emergency management. No one's perfect. Individuals and organizations have a better chance of success in a crisis when they put operational goals ahead of themselves. Forget your ego and focus on the mission.

CHOOSE COORDINATION OVER CONTROL

I once worked with an emergency manager who always had to be the smartest person in the room. During interagency meetings, he would pontificate on every agenda topic. He criticized other agencies for their work and tended to rehash old issues dealt with years ago. He wanted to control everything until something went wrong.

Younger colleagues in the business avoided him. They called him "the pompous pest." They hesitated to bring him issues because he had a reputation for blaming the messenger. As a result, he was constantly out of the loop on emerging problems.

The thing was, he was intelligent, organized, and had good ideas; but his disruptive and controlling style turned everyone off. He was impossible to collaborate with to resolve concerns. When other organizations assembled thought leaders and after-action groups to tackle problems, they avoided contacting this guy's agency. They didn't want him to end up on their team.

Few actions contribute more to crisis failure than misunderstanding the relationship between coordination and control. The more leaders try to control during a crisis, the less power they have. If you try to control everything, you will end up controlling nothing.

The word "coordinating" appears forty-six times in The Robert T. Stafford Disaster Relief and Emergency Assistance Act, which establishes the foundation for national responses for most disasters. "Controlling" doesn't merit a mention. "Coordination" appears seventy-five times, and "control" only forty times.

While "coordination" usually refers to interagency decision-making processes, "control," when used, often refers to ownership of a facility, business, or resource—for example, the requirement for "fraud controls" or the name of a piece of legislation, such as The Fire Control Act or the ironically named Flood Control Act. (Isn't a flood, by definition, an out-of-control overflow of water?)

The term "control" has a different connotation in the emergency management discipline, and this semantic difference is worth noting. "Control in emergency management often refers to the limits of the command authority of an individual or agency," according to training material produced by the Emergency Management Institute.

The Stafford Act, the National Incident Management System (NIMS), and international emergency management principles recognize that commanding a calamity requires helping diverse organizations and personalities come together to implement shared crisis priorities. You do this by creating functioning teams, asking for help, delegating responsibilities, and respecting the technical capabilities of responding entities. To gain control, you must give up control.

I've seen emergency managers build collaborative teams merely by conducting impromptu stand-up huddles, taking advantage of hallway exchanges to get feedback, and walking around and sharing their mission objectives. When individuals from other organizations arrive to assist them, they help the newcomers succeed by acknowledging their expertise, defining their mission, and welcoming them. They don't act threatened.

You can become a renowned, respected, and influential expert in emergency management not by being a condescending know-it-all but by being mission-focused, eager to learn, and dedicated to building relationships. Moreover, every disaster should be viewed as a chance to assist with the current incident and improve the nation's capability to deal with the next one. Emergency managers have a responsibility to use every available opportunity to strengthen each other. It should never be a competition.

When you fight for control in emergency management, you lose an opportunity to coordinate. The mission, and many future disasters, suffer as a result. In emergency management, coordination trumps control.

BE A PRIORITY GATEKEEPER

Sometimes, emergency managers have ambitious ideas to help during disaster recovery, but we forget that the infrastructure might not be in place to support them. Stay focused on the priorities and don't get sidetracked.

In 2015, I served a short stint as the federal tribal liaison officer to the Oglala Sioux Tribe of the Pine Ridge Indian Reservation following a flood disaster. I was vacation relief for the primary officer, FEMA's Megan Floyd. "You need to be a gatekeeper," Megan instructed me. "Everyone needs decisions from the tribe, but you need to help collect those requests, triage them, and match them with the tribe's priorities. Don't make decisions for them, but collect information, organize it, and share it with the tribe."

Within a day, I discovered what Megan meant. An official called me from another federal agency. "We have a recovery grant opportunity, and the tribe might have a chance to get it," he said. I asked him for details. He emailed me a twenty-page application. The requirements for the application included a narrative summary, grant proposal, accompanying statistics, management plan, and reporting procedures.

"I need to talk to the tribal emergency management office right away about this," he said. "It's a great opportunity. The emergency office just has to gather top department heads, reserve a conference room for thirty people, and arrange a meeting. And, by the way, we'll need a large screen and a projector."

At the time, Del Brewer comprised the entire full-time tribal emergency management office, and his priority was to support the most extensive emergency housing operation in the tribe's history. As federally-contracted repair crews prepared to fix flood-damaged homes, Del's job was to find each family a temporary place to live during the repairs. He had hundreds of families on his list. When I debriefed him on the grant offer, he said, "Maybe later. I don't have time right now." The tribe would have to divert resources to apply for it, which would have delayed the recovery of families waiting for safe housing. The guy thought the tribe was making a mistake by postponing his meeting when, in fact, it was trying not to jeopardize its first priority.

DON'T ASSUME YOU ARE FAILING

Sometimes you can get into your head, thinking you're on the verge of a screw-up when you're not.

For several years, I worked on assignments for NATO as a US Liaison Representative for civil emergency planning. One day, NATO called me and asked me to fly to Brussels to be part of a planning committee called COIAT—Consequences of Missile Intercept Analysis Team. Their job was to determine the impact on people and communities if an attack missile was blown up in the sky.

I arrived in Brussels for my first meeting and was immediately introduced to the twelve physicists, nuclear engineers, and rocket scientists who made up the team at that time. That was apparently NATO's idea: twelve scientists and me, a PIO from FEMA. I couldn't figure out how I ended up on this team and didn't have a clue what they were talking about.

I sat with them for the entire four days. I concentrated really hard, paid attention, and took copious notes. Nothing. At the end of the week, before departing from NATO headquarters, I went to my advisors at the US mission office.

"Look," I said. "I really appreciate this opportunity. But I got to tell you, I think there's been a mistake. Maybe there are two Ed Conleys in your system—some scientist from MIT and me—and we got mixed up."

"Hold on, hold on," one of my advisors said. "Maybe if you don't know what they are talking about, there are others who don't either. And when you figure it out, then you can come back and tell the rest of us."

"I don't know," I said dubiously.

"Look," he told me. "You're underestimating yourself. There's been no mistake. Think about where you can fit in:

- There's obviously an emergency management component. That's your background. Share your perspective.
- Public alert and warning needs to be a component of any intercept response. That's your area of expertise. Contribute your ideas.
- Look at opportunities for internal communications. Help

communicate the progress of this initiative with the rest of us."

It was one of the best assignments I had in my twenty-seven-year FEMA career. I spent parts of three years on the team. I even ended up preparing the official record after each of the team's regular meetings. What I thought was going to be a failure was the exact opposite. I learned a lot, made great friends, worked with brilliant people, and, I believe, made a contribution to the cause.

CONSIDER FEEDBACK A GIFT

In an *onlinecollege.org* blog post, Katina Solomon compiled "50 Famously Successful People Who Failed at First." Her list includes Henry Ford, Soichiro Honda, Bill Gates, Walt Disney, Albert Einstein, Thomas Edison, Abraham Lincoln, Oprah Winfrey, Harry Truman, Sidney Poitier, Emily Dickinson, J.K. Rowling, and Michael Jordan. Try to see any professional screw-up not as a failure but as an instructive setback, a learning experience, and maybe even an opportunity.

An emergency manager I worked for said it perfectly: "Feedback is a gift." Disasters require flexibility and adjustments. It's easy to surround yourself with nodding sycophants blaming "fake news" and politics for setbacks.

A genuine crisis—not a manufactured political crisis or a self-inflicted personal one, but a catastrophic flood, terrorist attack, or devastating earthquake—will have life-altering consequences for people and communities. Responders must make many initial decisions quickly with partial information. Inevitably, they make changes as their disaster intelligence improves.

If you welcome feedback, especially from those you're assisting, it can actually improve your response. Criticism often indicates that things aren't going right and that you must adjust. In a crisis, you want to work with people who aren't afraid of the situation or setbacks. Those who prove particularly adept at mitigating failure consider feedback a gift.

None of us will avoid experiencing career setbacks, missteps, and failures. Yet, when professional adversity strikes, we all have access to valuable tools, tactics, lessons, and friends. With these resources and the right mindset, you can not only overcome failure, but also learn from it and use it to your advantage.

CHAPTER 8

Talk Straight

HOW TO EARN PUBLIC TRUST

"I am a firm believer in the people. If given the truth, they can be depended upon to meet any national crisis. The great point is to bring them the real facts."

—ABRAHAM LINCOLN

Destruction in the Lower Ninth Ward of New Orleans after the levees failed following Hurricane Katrina (September 2005). Photo by Andrea Booher/FEMA.

In the 1983 movie, *The Right Stuff*, one of the Mercury Seven Astronauts asked a gathering of NASA scientists if they knew what made their spaceships fly. The scientists paused as if thinking.

"They do," the astronaut said, pointing to the reporters off to the side.

He meant that public support and funding for the mission, more than lift, thrust, or fuel, made the spacecraft fly.

The emergency management system also depends on having the trust and credibility of the public.

When the system works well, local, state, territorial, and tribal governments work with the private sector, volunteers, and federal responders to coordinate efforts, share resources, and avoid duplication. There is unified leadership with shared priorities. Responders rescue and shelter survivors and help communities rebuild. Congress supports them within the system. The media challenges, questions, and holds agencies accountable instead of destroying their credibility. And most importantly, individuals and communities take charge of their recovery. Survivors know what to expect regarding how long their recovery might take, understand what help is and is not available, and have been told what they need to do to manage their comeback.

Unfortunately, our emergency management system hasn't always worked as it should, particularly when leaders create—or fail to address—the public information gap between expectation and reality.

How do you communicate with disaster survivors, protect

your organization's long-term credibility, and earn public trust during a crisis? By talking straight.

SETTING REALISTIC EXPECTATIONS

In the 1990s, the emergency management community adopted the catchphrase "Government disaster assistance can help, but it won't make you whole." This message emphasized an important truth: there are limits to what governments can do after large-scale catastrophes. Individuals and communities also need to take charge of their own recovery.

When FEMA joined the newly-created Department of Homeland Security (DHS) in 2003, however, this talking point was quickly shelved for several reasons.

1. As the new administration filled national emergency management positions, they often selected former elected officials and political advisors. Many of these new leaders seemed uncomfortable using the "we can't make you whole" messaging because it sounded negative. They also didn't have context, as they had never managed large-scale, multiyear recovery operations.

2. The newcomers didn't believe the message was needed. They would point to the public support emergency managers had garnered during the late 1990s and in the aftermath of 9/11. In many ways, 9/11 represented the high-water mark regarding FEMA's national reputation. One agency employee told me that while flying home from New York, the aircraft captain announced that he was on board, and everyone on the plane broke out in applause. In the eyes of the new leadership, the national emergency management system was

working. Setting realistic expectations didn't appear to be an issue.

3. Other messages had higher priority. With the establishment of DHS, departmental leadership encouraged new talking points that played up the value of the new DHS, including the benefits of disaster response.

Public expectations for disaster response capabilities appeared in line with reality. The emergency management system looked ready to rock and roll regardless of what might happen next. Encouraging public support for DHS made sense because that credibility would help the department be even more successful.

However, this overconfidence and emphasis on reassurance quickly led to message creep. One day in 2003, while I was in Guam working on the Typhoon Pongsona response, our mainland colleagues sent us a copy of an article in the LA Times. It described FEMA's move into DHS and reported on "fears" from the emergency management community that this "will reduce [the agency's] focus on response to such disasters as earthquakes."

The response from a senior emergency management official mentioned our current operation in Guam. "My instructions, as in the past, were, 'Get these people on their feet, just fix it, make them whole again.' It was just as it has always been."

Whoops.

In my experience as a federal responder, these outsized promises frustrate community leaders. As one local responder pointed out, "You know what happens. People hear stuff like this. They remember it. Then your federal agencies wrap up your recovery activities and head home or off to the next disaster. After you leave, we're on the hot seat, having to explain years later why people got less help than the government led them to believe they would."

"We can't give disaster survivors the impression we can wave a magic wand and make everything all right. When those false hopes crash, recovery stalls out," he added.

Is there help available? Yes. Hope for the future? Also yes. Can you come back stronger? You can. But will the government make you whole like before the disaster? No. It can't. It doesn't. It never does.

"It's better to set realistic expectations," one crisis leader told me. "It takes communities ten years or more to recover from big disasters. That's a long, tough, muddy road trip. Yet you can get there with help, encouragement, perseverance, and when the directions are good."

Emergency management officials must encourage people to work with all responding organizations and utilize available resources. You have to remember, however, that nothing will replace everything people lost, including the lives of loved ones and community members. Remind people that government assistance will support the recovery but that it's up to individuals and communities to manage and complete their comeback.

THE OPPOSITE OF REALISTIC EXPECTATIONS

If you were a disaster survivor, wouldn't you want to know the facts instead of false hopes? Yet some crisis leaders still over-promise. Why?

It's usually for one of these seven reasons.

1. They give in to impulses for self-promotion. People love to announce the good news.
2. They worry about how people will react to bad news.
3. They underestimated the scope of the disaster.
4. They have overestimated the government's capabilities to respond to the disaster.
5. They lack the crisis experience or political motivation that drives decisions rather than science or best practices.
6. They didn't put themselves in the position of a survivor. What do they need to hear instead of want to hear?
7. They hold a sincere belief that emergency managers will somehow make their promises come true.

Compounding these are other factors:

- Disasters are too unpredictable to know the extent of the damage as it unfolds. You may be dealing with one and get hit by another.
- It's impossible to fully predict how catastrophes may impact people, what help they need, and how quickly you can get it to them.
- It's getting harder to anticipate the scope of disasters. As population growth continues in high-risk areas, new threats continue to emerge, and the implications of climate change are only beginning to be understood.

You'll never be able to deliver the right amount of assistance at the right time, exactly when needed. You can overpromise and likely harm the recovery, or you can let people know the full extent of the challenges and limitations they face.

The realistic expectation takeaways here:

- Crisis leaders must acknowledge they cannot guarantee anything during a disaster.
- You cannot break promises that erode trust in your leadership and organization, as the public will then perceive authorities as dishonest or less capable.
- You can't expect survivors to address, plan, and work on their recovery with partial, incomplete, or inaccurate information.

Now that we've looked at the *why*, let's examine the *how*.

HOW CRISIS LEADERS CREATE AN INFORMATION GAP

Crisis leaders want to help, but they sometimes get in their own way. For instance:

- **They overpromise help.** For example, officials publicize the number of emergency shelters available for use before the staff has opened and stocked them.
- **They minimize the event.** This occurs when managers don't have all the facts or decide not to share them with the public. Not being clear about an imminent threat or the disaster's potential can result in even more lives being lost. It can also damage the credibility of responding organizations.
- **They aren't transparent.** For example, crisis leadership does

not tell people the truth about what they will need to do independently. They may also hide their mistakes or miscalculations, resulting in unexpected delays.

The consequences can make it difficult for survivors to manage their recovery.

A COMMUNITY PERSPECTIVE ON REALISTIC EXPECTATIONS

In June 2011, Minot and Burlington, ND, suffered a devastating flood. Like New Orleans during Hurricane Katrina, and Grand Forks in 1997, floodwaters overtopped the levees.

North Dakota was booming due to the oil shale industry, and Minot, the larger of the two communities, had become a hub for commerce and housing. Before the flood, the city already had a near-zero percent vacancy rate on rental property. Then the flood wiped out 25 percent of the housing, displacing a large portion of the area's population.

The nearest town to Minot was Bismarck, 110 miles away, so people could not simply move to the next town. North Dakota winters also come quickly and last long. A late June flood provided limited opportunities to build new housing until the following year. That meant the most significant crisis following the flood was where people would live.

FEMA had a program that provided manufactured housing units to keep families near their original homes. This emergency housing strategy allowed people to remain in their communities with jobs, schools, and existing lives while rebuilding their damaged homes.

It takes time to set the program up, however. FEMA had to bring the mobile homes to the area, access locations, adhere to local requirements, and build the infrastructure to support them, including water, sewer, and power. Families who lost their homes were understandably anxious, as were local officials under incredible pressure to help their citizens. To reassure people and pressure the Army Corps of Engineers assigned to building the group sites, a government official publicly promised that families would start moving in September.

Unfortunately, some units were unavailable until November, and families were still moving around Christmas.

As one city leader told me:

> The problem with the September date is that people grabbed hold of that and made decisions based on that time frame. Huge decisions. Decisions about where to live, a job in a different city, and where to enroll their kids in school. Some families had babies on the way; winter was coming, and they could not live in a damaged home now. If we had known the actual length of time, it would have been helpful as we planned our recovery. Yes, at first, we might have been disappointed—even angry—but it would have been the best thing for us. You have to know this.

The final time frame was reasonable. The government made a significant effort to ensure the units were safe and secure, including burying water and sewer lines eight feet down to avoid North Dakota's winter freeze. They brought in two thousand mobile homes and turned open fields into mini-cities with roads, infrastructure, and housing for thousands of people within a few months. It was the federal government's second-largest mobile home program since Hurricane Katrina (after Hurricane Ike) and was a success. It would have been even more so if the government had not initially set expectations so high.

IF YOU CAN'T BE PERFECT, BE HONEST

Even when you have initially overpromised, you can reset the public's expectations by being transparent.

Morrie Goodman and Phil Cogan taught me to identify and publicize internal operational mistakes early in my FEMA career. If you find something your organization did wrong, don't wait to share this information, especially in a disaster. Let people know and tell them how you intend to fix it. In crisis recovery, credibility is critical to maintaining public trust. Few people expect responding organizations to be perfect, but everyone expects them to be honest. Bad news will eventually get out and torpedo your credibility if you're the last to talk about it.

CORRECTING AN OVERPROMISE

In 1995, the government deployed me to St. Thomas in the US Virgin Islands after Hurricane Marilyn. We had been expecting the arrival of a large cargo ship carrying desperately needed blue roof tarps, baby formula, construction material, food, and water.

I worked with Phil Cogan as part of the federal-territory joint communications team. We had made the unfortunate mistake of announcing what day we had intended to move supplies to various distribution centers. We had broken a cardinal rule in disaster operations: never promise when something will be available. Wait until you have it, then tell people it is available.

The night before the ship's expected arrival, we learned choppy seas had delayed it. We knew thousands of people would be lined up outside the centers under a boiling sun waiting for supplies the following day.

"Just to let you know," one center manager told me, "all we have right now is a few tarps and many hammers. People will show up tomorrow expecting food and water, and we'll pass out hammers."

I've seen crisis managers facing a similar dilemma use the "do nothing" strategy. They believed calling attention to the mistake would only make people angrier. The best leaders, in my experience, acknowledge the problem, accept responsibility, announce a solution, and follow up.

Phil Cogan chose to handle it by going on the radio, giving a heads-up to a few others in the operation. Some pushed back, fearing locals would get angry and start rioting. Phil stood his ground. President Clinton's designee on the island, Federal Coordinating Officer Dennis Kwiatkowski, ultimately agreed that it was a good idea to "go ahead and let people know."

There was only one operating radio station on the island: WSTA 1340 AM. "The Lucky 13" ran 24/7 and was the primary source of emergency information. At 10 p.m., Phil called the station and asked for time on the air with an important announcement.

"The relief supplies we expected tomorrow have been delayed," he said, asking for patience. "They won't be available tomorrow. Please help us let people know. We're sorry for the delay, but we must let you know. We don't want people to stand outside all day waiting for nothing. The ship is still coming, and we will announce it as soon as supplies are here."

Most got the word, and staff at the centers quickly informed those who didn't. They also gave people the news immediately instead of letting them be surprised at the end of the line. Many were sad and disappointed, but nothing like an uncontrolled mob charging the doors.

Within a few days, the supply chain was going full-throttle. Phil's apology also helped us build better relationships with survivors on St. Thomas. They knew the news wouldn't always be good but that we would be straight. People can manage their recoveries better when they know what to expect.

Long-time emergency management leader Mary Hudak suggests that the best way to frame communications is to ensure your public messaging dovetails with operational realities. "In a disaster, let operations drive your words, your public messaging. Don't fall into the trap of thinking your words will drive operations. Emergency communications during a crisis should follow—and support—operations, not the other way around."

If you promise specifics on what *will*, *should*, or *might* happen, you may be overpromising. If you stick to describing what's currently happening, you'll stay on track.

PROCEDURES, TOOLS, AND MODELS FOR TALKING STRAIGHT

Federal, state, and local public information officers from law enforcement and emergency management agencies coordinate public safety messaging during the 2008 Democratic National Convention in Denver, Colorado. Photo by Michael Rieger/FEMA.

The emergency management community takes public communications seriously during a crisis. Governors and jurisdictions in hurricane-, wildfire-, and flood-prone states use established guidance when making evacuation decisions. They use science-based forecast projections from meteorology agencies. Their policies also include decison-related trigger points and pre-scripted public messages written for actual circumstances. Law enforcement must evaluate whether releasing information to the public will compromise an investigation or alter the threat, possibly increasing the risk to the public, including for national security events.

When communicating the threat during an emergency, the primary goals are to:

- achieve maximum public protection;
- provide actionable information to individuals, families, and organizations;
- help the public make decisions appropriate for their situation; and
- ask for action from the public so responders can concentrate efforts where needs are greatest.

In addition to these models:

- The federal government's Emergency Support Function (ESF) #15 provides coordination and organizational guidance. It also incorporates policy established in Presidential Policy Directive-8, Homeland Security Presidential Directive-5, the National Response Framework, National Incident Management System (NIMS), and the Incident Command System.
- The Centers for Disease Control and Prevention has emergency public information messaging guidance in its Crisis and Emergency Risk Communications Manual.
- FEMA has published the NIMS Basic Guidance for Public Information Officers.
- Other federal agencies, states, tribal nations, territorial offices, local governments, the private sector, and humanitarian relief organizations publish disaster communication principles.

Governments often revise emergency information policies after—or in anticipation of—incidents of major significance. For instance:

- The federal government adopted incident organizational

and interagency coordination practices under the ESF #15 structure after Hurricane Katrina.

- Following the 9/11 terrorist attacks, the federal government issued Homeland Security Presidential Directive5, referencing public communications.
- In 2007, as pandemic planning intensified, "HSPD-21: Public Health and Medical Preparedness" included establishing a United States policy to "plan and enable the provision for the public health and medical needs of the American people in the case of a catastrophic health event through continual and timely information during such an event."

HISTORICAL MODELS

If you look at Winston Churchill's most famous WWII speeches, he often used a three-step process to communicate by identifying key ideas:

- **The Challenge:** let the public know you understand what people are experiencing.
- **What Needs To Be Done:** describe what it will take to overcome the challenge.
- **The Outcome:** describe the result when everyone does their part, stays focused on common goals, and implements the plan.

More than a quarter-century after President Clinton's April 22, 1997 speech to Grand Forks evacuees and relief workers, locals still quote the essence of Clinton's remarks. He said:

I saw something your mayor said the other day, and it stuck with me in particular. She said, 'What makes a community a place to live in is not the buildings, it's the people, and the spirit and the faith that are in those people.' Water cannot wash that away. Fire cannot burn that away. A blizzard cannot freeze that away. And if you don't give that away, it will bring you back better than ever. And we'll be with you every step of the way.

Clinton shared what he learned about dealing with adversity from the community, emphasizing that the community had it right. He acknowledged the devastation the community had suffered and what it needed to do moving forward. He also said that if the community did their part, the government would do its part—that "we'll be with you."

We can't all be as inspirational, but we can be clear, be straight, use the right words, and maximize the power of public communications during disasters. The procedures and documents listed above are great resources for that.

In addition, when you hear a good speech or memorable sound-bite, evaluate it from the frame of an emergency manager. Look at the phrasing and how the speaker structured the themes of challenges, set honest expectations, and talked about help and hope. What words did they use? When you hear something that touches you, it will likely resonate with others, too.

DESPITE HAVING GOOD COMMUNICATION MODELS, WE DON'T ALWAYS USE THEM

With all these tools, you may wonder why emergency public communications on occasion seems left to chance or to spur-of-the-moment judgment calls.

Despite recognition that health, safety, and recovery information is essential when dealing with any emergency, crisis leaders sometimes provide it haphazardly. Three reasons:

1. They don't use guiding principles.
2. They don't use existing decision-making models for communications.
3. They rely on inexperienced advisors (or experienced advisors who don't speak up).

Leaders who do not have a strong foundation in these three areas often wing it during a crisis. As a result, they may over-promise, minimize risk, and hide things from the public. Furthermore, inexperienced crisis leaders have a tendency to disregard existing communications models when dealing with an event that is new or unprecedented, especially if they are unsure how the public will react to bad news.

Perhaps nothing illustrates that tendency better than the assumption that "the public will panic." When leaders think the public might panic, they often do the opposite of what they do during other types of emergencies.

WHY DO WE ASSUME THE PUBLIC WILL PANIC DURING A CRISIS?

In 2016, the federal government conducted a crisis planning seminar for leadership of federal, state, tribal, and local emergency management organizations in Denver, Colorado. During one module, the trainers said public panic was a vital planning concept during unprecedented events. "Be prepared for this," one instructor said solemnly. He then played a clip of a panicked crowd—from the 1996 science fiction movie *Independence Day*.

"People will panic" is a common assumption held by responders, community leaders, the media, and even presidents. Many in the audience watching the video with me that day nodded in agreement. No one challenged the instructor. Behavioral scientists would argue they should have.

In studying numerous disasters, fires, plane crashes, and terrorist attacks over fifty years, Rutgers University Professor of Sociology Lee Clarke found this oft-repeated belief underestimates the ability of people to handle even the most horrendous life-threatening situations.

In a crisis, genuine mass panic is rare. Fear, however, can be reasonable, leading people to make rational decisions that keep them safe, such as evacuating the Twin Towers after the 9/11 terrorist attacks, climbing up a canyon during a flash flood, or rushing inland during a tsunami.

On January 13, 2018, an employee at the Hawaii Emergency Management Agency pressed the wrong button on the state's alert system during an exercise and sent a statewide warning of an imminent ballistic missile inbound to Hawaii. In less than an hour, the government corrected this information, but by then, people scrambled for shelter, called loved ones, and huddled with their families in bathtubs. Reporters said the false alarm caused "mass and widespread panic." It didn't.

People were scared. Some may have even described themselves

as "panicky, terrified, and crying." Yet, the threat of a missile attack on Hawaii is real enough that the state conducted regular drills for that scenario. The false message, issued from official government sources to the cell phones of a million people, had the presence of truth.

To suggest the entire state lost its head is a disservice to the islands' crisis management heritage, including the Pearl Harbor attack, the devastating 1949 tsunami, and Hurricane Iniki in 1992. Most people did things that made sense, like finding shelter or caring for their children. According to reporters Julia Carrie Wong and Liz Barney, Joshua Keoki Versola figured he'd go out in style "and opened a bottle of Hibiki 21, an expensive Japanese whiskey."

Professor Clarke points out that from his research, people in a disaster are "often models of civility and cooperation." We teach people to believe the worst in people during a crisis. In truth, you'll see many at their best. Clarke's advice: "Don't pacify. Inform."

BUILDING PUBLIC TRUST BY TRUSTING THE PUBLIC

Government leaders have cited concerns about mass panic when deciding how to discuss the scope of a threat. Usually, this leads to withholding or minimizing health and safety information, believing it will prevent more significant harm. However, it is unclear on what historical evidence or research crisis leaders based these concerns.

Between 2005 and 2008, the Department of Homeland Security External Affairs initiated an effort to study the correlation between emergency public messaging and public reaction. At the time, the department's posture indicated an overall government trend toward early engagement with the public during imminent threats, based on lessons learned from the 9/11 terrorist attacks and Hurricane Katrina.

Lee Clarke's 2002 landmark crisis response study "Panic: Myth or Reality?" also impressed DHS. The study concluded that:

- In a crisis, mass panic is rare.
- The public is more willing to act on official instructions during an emergency.
- The most common public reactions are often civility and cooperation when the trouble begins.

Though additional research has drawn similar conclusions, many crisis decision-makers have not incorporated this knowledge into their procedures.

Panic avoidance was cited as a government messaging goal during the 1918 influenza pandemic. As mentioned in Chapter 7, it was a reason local weather forecasters were not allowed to issue forecasts before the 1900 Galveston Hurricane. In 2020, President Trump, in a meeting with reporters, "acknowledged that he downplayed the novel coronavirus earlier this year, arguing he wanted to 'reduce panic' about the spreading disease by publicly minimizing its threat," according to an account of the meeting published in *The Hill*. "I don't want people to be frightened. I don't want people to panic," the president reportedly said.

These aren't the only examples of panic assumptions in the emergency management industry. An April 2022 Google-driven review of leadership guidance for disasters and public health emergencies found "planning for mass panic" references in governmental and non-governmental publications. For instance, "Control of traffic and panic" appears on page seventy-nine of the Stafford Act, as Amended, as a government responsibility during a hazard.

Crisis leaders must evaluate the public's assumptions and set realistic expectations when needed. That's crucial in any response. But making communication decisions based on misperceptions about how the public may react can lead to real problems. If the government hopes to earn public trust during crises, it must first trust the public.

PRACTICE TALKING STRAIGHT DAILY

You might be surprised how often you already practice the principle of talking straight to the public. How often do you tell your family or friends about your job or your organization's mission? Even in everyday encounters, you have opportunities to set realistic expectations.

During a crisis, think about how often you communicate with people outside your organization, even in informal situations. It could be at the airport, a hotel, a restaurant, or during an impromptu face-to-face with a community leader. All those encounters add up.

There's another level of responsibility, too. As an emergency management professional, part of your job involves:

- helping your organization anticipate decision points in public trust messaging;

- helping your leadership understand the consequences of communication decisions; and
- providing examples of how leaders handled those decisions during other disasters.

When leadership messaging looks out-of-whack with reality, offer your thoughts with concrete recommendations.

History is littered with crisis incidents where responders knew their leadership had misstated facts, set unrealistic expectations, and sometimes outright lied. Sometimes employees stood up and challenged their leadership, and sometimes they didn't. As an emergency manager, you're expected to do the right thing even if it's really hard.

For instance, chime in if you're in a planning meeting and the boss mentions the importance of avoiding public panic. Challenge the statement. Suggest options. Provide examples. Don't let the panic assumption default to an automatic conclusion. This decision could result in withholding life-saving information, potentially causing more harm during any response.

ADOPTING THE TALK STRAIGHT PRINCIPLE

Consider whether you need a personal commitment to public communications. You could call it "Your Personal Compact on Emergency Public Information." The idea is to have a framework in your mind of how to talk straight during a crisis.

Several themes emerge when studying the existing tools, procedures, and documents referenced earlier in the chapter. These have been echoed by national leaders, governors, mayors, tribal nations, agency heads, non-elected informal community leaders, and disaster survivors in times of crisis.

- Successful crisis leaders recognize that emergency public information is as vital as food, water, medical care, and shelter.
- The public expects emergency public information that is timely, accurate, credible, accessible, actionable, and based on the best available science, data, and practices learned from previous disasters.
- Emergency public information is readily available, quickly activated, and incredibly consequential as a government resource. However, it is uniquely vulnerable to mismanagement that can result in further public harm.
- The most critical role of a leader during a crisis is to earn and maintain the public's trust. Public trust engenders coordination and cooperation.
- Emergency public information is the foundation for building public trust. Leaders should communicate the full extent of the threat, resources available to address it, limitations to meeting emergency needs, how they will address shortfalls, and the public's role in mitigating the consequences of a crisis.

Sharing the bad and the ugly, as well as the good, takes a concerted effort during a crisis. Yet, ultimately, people will respect and appreciate that you cared enough to look out for their long-term best interest rather than "sparing their feelings" in the moment. Your goal is to help communities rise to resilience. And they need to prepare for challenges they may face along the way. Never underestimate how much people rely on trustworthy information throughout the recovery journey.

CHAPTER 9

Follow Up

HOW TO HONOR YOUR PROMISES

"Many people don't focus enough on execution. If you make a commitment to get something done, you need to follow through on that commitment. For me, integrity is the consistency of words and action."

—KENNETH CHENAULT

A disaster welfare strike team visits a Superstorm Sandy survivor in New York City's Coney Island neighborhood on November 20, 2012. Photo by Andrea Booher/FEMA.

During the Northridge Earthquake, Steve Olsen helped manage the federal Community Relations program, a new initiative by James Lee Witt to increase the agency's field presence during disasters. The teams identified emerging issues for the response agencies and provided emergency information to survivors. They also organized community meetings.

A community organizer approached Witt, who had spoken at the event, outside the auditorium following one session. The FEMA Chief of Staff, Bill Tidball, was with Witt. As their conversation continued, I saw Tidball glance over to where I was standing with Steve and a group of ten other FEMA Community Relations staff. Tidball's eyes scanned across our group and beckoned for Steve, who rushed to their side and leaned in, furiously scribbling notes.

The next day, I saw him work the phone and visit multiple program offices to find answers to the community organizer's questions. He then called this person on behalf of Witt and gave him the information. Then he caught up with FEMA's Tidball to close the loop.

I can't remember any of the information James Lee asked Steve to collect. Yet more than a quarter of a century later, I vividly remember how importantly he treated this assignment. Witt had made a promise to follow up. He assigned that to Steve, who went right to work and didn't stop until he made good on it. I later learned how valued that effort is within emergency management.

As a crisis leader, part of your goal is building positive long-term relationships. That means demonstrating credibility to earn trust. As a crisis leader I once worked with used to say, "If you want loyalty, be loyal." You want to create trust and participation, and encourage people to jump on board. You do this by making your words matter. If you say you'll do something, do it.

EMBRACE THE FAITH OTHERS PUT IN YOU

Early in my FEMA career, one of my mentors was John Swanson. John had played football at Colorado State University and, even in his fifties, projected the confidence and grace of a Division One college athlete. In 1996, John asked me to develop a multimedia presentation on the Big Thompson Canyon Flood. He was the keynote speaker at a symposium commemorating the twentieth anniversary. It was the first time he had asked me to do something for him. Of course, I said yes.

From the beginning, I procrastinated. I didn't know where to start. I had a grand vision for the product but couldn't get any pieces together. Other things came up. I told myself that John would understand. Or, even better, maybe he'd forget he had asked me. I convinced myself he probably had his presentation ready to go independently.

I had a few things to learn about the crisis response business. When people demonstrate faith and confidence in your ability, you don't treat that lightly. If you want to be the type of employee—or leader—that people rely on, show them that you are one.

Two weeks before the event, John asked me how it was coming along, and I told him I hadn't started. He looked at me for a long time. "You let me down," he said. "You've disappointed me."

It was gut-wrenching criticism. I immediately dropped everything, canceled sleeping, and begged other staff for help. In a week, I managed to pull together a professional-looking presentation. The documentary featured powerful images and interviews with responders and survivors from the disaster, set to music. I was actually proud of it. I completed the project a few days before the symposium. But I never saw it delivered in front of an audience. The day after I turned it in, John and I got deployed to South Carolina in advance of Hurricane Bertha. Another staffer gave the presentation.

Though things turned out well that time, I vowed to do my best never to short-circuit a follow-up commitment again. Disappointing someone I admired made me feel so horrible that I became obsessed with following up. It's essential to do; and yet it's also so easy to blow something—or someone—off. A follow-up is a personal commitment.

Imagine you are talking to a survivor at a community meeting. They ask you a question. You say you'll check and get back to them, but you never do. We've all had that customer service experience when someone says they'll call you back and you never hear from them again. In emergency management, this commitment is even more meaningful. Think about the organization you represent—perhaps their government—and the vulnerable position of the other person. You'll probably never see them again. They don't know how to contact you.

This typical interaction relates to the last principle of not overpromising. Both establish your credibility and, by extension, the credibility of the organization you represent. Don't promise to follow up if you cannot follow through.

Decades ago, at a San Francisco conference, I listened to the late Robert Waterman Jr., who studied business management strategies.

"I was talking to leadership at an automotive company," Waterman told the audience. "A senior executive said to me, 'Now, at our company, quality is job one.'

"I said, 'Wait a minute. You've been saying that for years.'

"'I know,' the executive replied. 'But this time, we really mean it.'"

People may not remember all the times you followed up, but it should be the standard that you did. Over time, you will build a reputation. When you say, "You have my word," there will be no doubt.

A BIG FOLLOW-UP IN EMERGENCY MANAGEMENT

Post-Katrina, a national consensus was that we needed to fix our emergency response system. As with all dramatic televised failures, the disaster generated its share of grandstanding politicians who offered criticism without solutions, delivered rehearsed soundbites to get a headline, and badgered dedicated public workers in showy congressional hearings.

Behind the scenes, however, there was also a team of legislative staffers working for the US Senate Committee on Homeland Security and Governmental Affairs, empowered by Senators Joe Lieberman and Susan Collins, who committed to understanding the problem. This team met with thousands of people and spoke with disaster survivors, local leaders, advocate groups, firefighters, state professionals, and experts in the field. One of the team members came to Colorado, where he met with emergency managers.

After the initial courtesy meeting with a few top regional leaders, where he received some vague and cautious recommendations, this guy stayed behind for another week. He met with program staff, front-line workers, and administrative assistants. He sought out people from state and local agencies. He met privately with those he judged had experience and were willing to share candid insights.

Congress was determined to create a legal framework for a more dynamic, nimble, and responsive national emergency management structure. If we didn't share our best ideas now, when would we ever have another chance? Changes were coming one way or another. If we didn't engage in the process, we would have to blame ourselves if we didn't like the results.

In the end, Congress passed the Post-Katrina Emergency Management Reform Act of 2006. Among other things, it established FEMA as a distinct agency within DHS, defined the agency's primary mission, and designated the FEMA Administrator as the principal advisor to the President and the Secretary of Homeland Security for all matters relating to emergency management in the US

Lawmakers followed up with further adjustments through the Sandy Recovery Improvement Act of 2013 (SRIA) and the Disaster Recovery Reform Act of 2018, using a similar process of listening to the experts. Congress passed these legislative initiatives to streamline public infrastructure recovery and increase mitigation opportunities. SRIA also allowed federally recognized Tribal Nations to directly request a presidential disaster declaration.

As emergency managers, we're often cynical of the legislative process. In these cases, Congress promised the nation, and they followed up.

THE EAGER BEAVERS WHO DON'T FOLLOW UP

There are two types of "eager beavers" in emergency management. The first kind believes saying something is the same as doing it. You might be able to get away with grandiose statements and unfulfilled promises of "I'll take care of that" in some professions. You can't be a successful crisis leader if you do that in emergency management.

The second type of "eager beaver" has ambitions exceeding their capabilities. Often, they can't admit their shortcomings or ask for help. They keep promising to do it soon. In most cases, they eventually give up, or it takes much longer than it should have.

Sometimes, however, things just looked more accessible than they were. A person who has embraced the follow-up principle adjusts when they can't fulfill their promise.

1. They let the other person know. They don't hide, lie, fake, or pretend, hoping the issue resolves itself.
2. They present a legitimate excuse if they have one.
3. They ask for more time or help.
4. They never allow the person to think the promise is coming when it is not.

Many people who complain about being "micromanaged" are the same people who make exaggerated promises to take care of something and then don't.

BETTER THAN GRAND INTENTIONS

One summer, FEMA assigned Andrea Booher, Jim Chesnutt, and me to document emergency management practices in Indian Country and identify opportunities for FEMA to assist the tribes in the Great Plains and Intermountain West.

By late August, we were on our way to share our perceived vast emergency management knowledge with the wildland firefighters from the remote Confederated Salish and Kootenai Tribes of the Flathead Nation, located north of Missoula, Montana, adjacent to the Missionary Mountains.

The crew we linked up with was part of the Montana Indian Firefighters group, known as the MIFFs.

Not far from the reservation, I crashed our car. It was my fault. We spotted a herd of bison running up a hill, and I slammed on the brakes to look. The car behind us didn't have time to stop and rammed into us. Before we even began our assignment with the tribe, I had screwed up. Tasked with teaching the Flathead Nation how to handle emergencies, I had instead created one. Now instead of helping the Indians, we needed them to help us.

Fortunately, the worst damage was to our rental car. The rear end crumbled. We felt okay, but more than a little shaken up, and more than a little lucky. We could have been pushed into the southbound lane and slammed by a semi-truck. We exchanged driver info and moved on.

We drove on the rez with rear lights smashed, the bumper hanging by zip cords, and the trunk roof flapping up and down. When we got there, no one from the tribe said a word about the car. No one asked what happened. And no one asked if we were okay.

Word travels fast on the reservation. The tribe knew about the crash right away, even before we had left the scene. And when we arrived, they saw the smashed-in rear of the car. But no one said a word about the accident.

After our meetings that day with the tribe, the MIFF crew boss, Basil "Baz" Tanner, invited Andrea and me to his house for dinner. He ran a rambunctious household, crowded with kids he had fathered and those he had adopted. We ate barbecued hamburgers and listened to stories about the family. He still hadn't mentioned the car crash.

Just before we left, Baz disappeared into the kitchen at the end of the evening. The smell of burning sage drifted through the room. Holding a frying pan with the sage ashes, Baz motioned us to come over. He took ashes from the pan and rubbed them on our foreheads. This ritual is an Indian prayer tradition called smudging, a healing practice. He did it because of the car accident.

"Now, you are protected," said Baz.

All day, because no one said a word about the car, we thought they didn't care much. It turned out they cared a lot. Baz considered us part of his team. As a firefighter, he paid attention to the health and safety of his crew, including knuckleheads like me. Baz embodied the Oscar Wilde wisdom that "The smallest act of kindness is worth more than the grandest intention."

The health and safety of responders is one of the first operational priorities in a crisis. If you don't protect the people charged with helping, they help no one and become another burden on the suffering community. As an elite response team, the MIFFs did this as well as anyone, in my opinion. And as we learned, it's one of many things Indian responders can teach the broader emergency management community.

The MIFF commitment to the health and safety promise was unspoken, but it was still a promise, and they followed up. They didn't say they were going to do it. They just did.

PROMISE MADE, PROMISE KEPT—HOWEVER LONG IT TOOK

When I taught at the Incident Management Assistance Team Academy in Anniston, Alabama, I often reminded new FEMA employees that they represented all of us in the agency, and the federal government, when they presented themselves to the outside world. With the privilege of serving the country comes responsibility, like following up.

I'd then tell them a story about two of their colleagues, the same Andrea Booher from the story above and Michael Rieger—the first two photographers granted twenty-four-hour access to Ground Zero in New York following the 9/11 terrorist attacks.

Their photographs and equipment, along with Jim Chesnutt's video documentation, reside in the Smithsonian Institution and Library of Congress. (I also used Andrea and Michael's photographs in this book, as you may have noticed.)

Andrea and Mike took thousands of photos. Every day, firefighters, police officers, chaplains, volunteers, medical personnel, contractors, and city employees would assist them in their efforts to document the events happening in lower Manhattan. Inevitably, Andrea and Mike would tell the responders they had photographed, "I'll send you a photo," and they did.

They kept individual notebooks of all their encounters: names, titles, and addresses. After their assignment ended, Andrea and Mike produced compilation CDs of their photographs. They sent these to all the people they had promised a photo to—including more than three thousand Ground Zero workers. It took them ten years to track down everyone they could. In 2011, they traveled back to New York for the tenth anniversary of the attacks and followed up some more—catching up with those they might have missed.

DEMONSTRATING FOLLOW-UP

In their 1982 book *In Search of Excellence: Lessons from America's Best-Run Companies,* Tom Peters and Robert Waterman Jr. offer leaders two follow-up techniques. Both techniques seem to work quite well in the emergency management industry. The first is the organizational stump speech. Successful leaders often use a short stump speech to employees to reemphasize their vision for the organization and how everyone connects to it, whether in a large meeting or in a one-on-one exchange in the cafeteria. This is similar to the leadership intent messaging we discussed in Chapter Three.

The second technique is the classic organizational theory, which they called Management by Wandering Around, or MBWA. They argued that managers should leave the comfort zones of their big desks and cushy offices, roam the hallways, and conduct the following types of actions:

- Drop in on sections.
- Talk to coworkers and ask questions.
- Get feedback.
- Listen to their challenges.
- Learn what people are working on and why they are working on it.
- Evaluate whether that effort coincides with the organizational or mission goals you've articulated.

One of the best bosses I ever had, Tim Deal, used to come by my office every morning and spend ten minutes leaning on the side of a table, just talking and listening. We would discuss projects we were working on and how those projects connected to our agency's mission. We'd speak about tactics one day and share big thoughts on organizational philosophy and the crisis response business the next. One of the best talks we had was about the lack of partnerships between disaster response practitioners and crisis management academics. Whatever the day's topic, Tim's visits were a high point that left me energized and motivated. He wasn't just a guy who talked about leadership theories. He demonstrated them. He followed up.

FOLLOW-UP DOESN'T JUST HAPPEN

Don't assume follow-up automatically occurs with the people you work with on an emergency management assignment. Often, you'll need to make sure your priorities are everyone's priorities.

I'm told that in the military, if a high-ranking commander enters a briefing center and casually mentions the walls are looking scruffy, the staff will have them repainted by the following day. The floors will sparkle with new polish.

We don't interpret offhanded remarks and casual observations as orders in emergency management. We do many things well—but, as my friend Justo Hernandez says, "We don't salute, and we don't march."

There's a good reason for this. Emergency management tends to be more collegial than the military, with a "first names" organizational culture. FEMA administrator Deanne Criswell is Deanne. Fugate is called Craig. We greet James Lee Witt as James Lee.

As coordinators, we require cooperation from other organizations to accomplish anything, and this coordination foundation is based on the laws that govern us. A more coordination-driven rather than hierarchical top-down culture means that if you want a follow-up, you may need to do it yourself or make clear it's a priority and follow it through the process.

Emergency management works closely with the military, and many former military members join emergency management organizations. So, it's worth keeping this cultural difference in mind.

TRACK YOUR FOLLOW-UP

One technique I've seen successful crisis leaders use is the notebook approach. Every time they committed to something, they wrote it down in their disaster notebook and marked it with a capital "A," meaning it was an action item. Then, as they followed up, they crossed off what they did and reviewed other commitments still open.

I also appreciate people who acknowledge emails. If someone sends you an action item, let them know you received it. If you can't complete the task, let the sender know. If you complete the assignment, close the loop. "As a crisis leader," one boss told me, "don't leave people hanging, wondering if their action request disappeared into a black hole. Let them know you got it, how you're handling it, and whether it got done."

No matter what tool you use, the key is staying focused on your priorities and your promises. Some crisis leaders do this exceptionally well. I worked with one manager who excelled at conducting productive meetings. One by one, she would tick off her priorities, demanding statistics, timeframes, problems, personal opinions, and accomplishments from all attendees. Once satisfied with the answers and reassured there was a plan in place, she'd move on to the next priority. She asked many questions and would repeat the solutions to make sure she'd heard them right.

Then at the next meeting, she would follow up. She had a great memory. Often, incident management meetings tend to be about reporting individual activities. This leader preferred to organize by issues. She wanted less to talk about what each person did today and more about what the collective team needed to fix. Things got done because no one wanted to admit to her that they didn't follow up.

WHEN THE FOLLOW-UP IS FAKE

I had several encounters with a former federal official who loved to talk about big ideas and champion future initiatives. One of his catchphrases was, "This is low-hanging fruit," meaning it was apparent, achievable, and actionable. During these encounters, he solicited employee feedback on operational and organizational improvements. At the time, I had been working with a former firefighter and ex-cop on a deployment reception center plan.

The federal government occasionally encounters large-scale disasters involving the deployment of thousands of people. In past events, staff deployed with unclear instructions, vague directions, no arrival contacts, and little understanding of the event itself, including safety instructions. Often, many of these responders were on their first disaster assignment.

In New York after Superstorm Sandy, I was charged with corralling hundreds of federal employees arriving at the Sheraton Brooklyn Hotel. They were the community relations force, whose job was to represent the federal government on the street in impacted neighborhoods.

Among hundreds of experienced staff, the workforce also included less capable hands who had somehow slipped through the deployment system. One woman had been diagnosed with possible early-onset Alzheimer's Disease, according to her daughter, who had come to keep "an eye on mom." I also received a call from a responder at LaGuardia airport who needed to know how to catch a cab in New York because this "was his first time in a big city."

I thought we could do better. In collaboration with my first responder cohorts, the former cop and the former firefighter, we designed a plan we presented several times to FEMA's future initiative point person. He told us our project sounded promising and that the problem we were addressing was an easy one to fix. "My after-action team will follow up with you," he said.

Months went by without any feedback, and then we had the opportunity to brief him on it a second time. He was again encouraging and seemed to like the concept. "We'll follow up on this with you," he repeated. "My team will get back to you guys on this." We waited, but they never did. We lost confidence in this guy and his staff after that.

SAYING YOU'LL DO IT IS NOT THE SAME AS ACTUALLY DOING IT

When FEMA became part of the Department of Homeland Security in 2003, senior administration officials wanted to reassure the emergency management community that the fledgling reorganization would benefit the agency and the nation. No one questioned the need to prepare for terrorism, but we still had to keep our eye on other things.

"We got your back; we're bigger and stronger than ever; now our federal response organizations are all around the same table" represented the messaging delivered by senior DHS officials to local communities in the first two-plus years after the department opened its doors in March 2003.

A high-ranking DHS political employee held an all-hands meeting with FEMA staff in mid-2005, a few months before Katrina. His message was that we should further support this reorganization.

"We're going to put FEMA on steroids," he said.

At the same time, DHS was considering folding FEMA into a subsection of the department, clamping down its previous independent status, and seemingly micromanaging agency decisions. DHS also placed an emphasis on branding the new department, even issuing a thirty-eight-page publication style guide to FEMA which included requirements on font types and color palettes.

Members of the public had their doubts as well. A year earlier, I ran into a homeowner just south of Denver while working on wildfires in Colorado. "You're too focused on terrorism," he warned. "You forget about the disasters like floods, fires, and hurricanes." He was right. The next big event of mass destruction wasn't another 9/11 attack. It was Hurricane Katrina.

Be cautious when people use powerful-sounding promise words. I'm immediately suspicious whenever I hear phrases like:

- We're going to "pivot" to a better position.
- We'll start looking at it through a new "prism."
- Fake News. (Whenever I hear this, my first reaction isn't to believe the news is fake, but that it's probably true.)
- We're making a paradigm shift.
- It's time to "think outside the box."
- We're going to do more with less. (A former colleague told

me every time he heard this one, he thought, "Oh no, I'm going to have to do everything with nothing.")

- "Don't let this be _____'s (insert politician's name here) Katrina." (I've heard this a lot. Attempting to motivate responders by instilling a fear of failure usually doesn't result in the outcome of success you desire.)

IN A CRISIS, WORDS MATTER, AND COMMITMENTS ARE REMEMBERED

In Season 2 of the comedy series *Seinfeld*, Jerry's neighbor Kramer announces a plan to redesign the inside of his apartment by building levels.

"Levels, Jerry," he says, pantomiming a series of platforms.

Jerry bets Kramer a dinner that he'll never complete the project.

"What, you don't think I can?" says Kramer, insulted.

"I am positive you won't," says Jerry.

Later, Jerry's dad asks Kramer how his levels are coming along.

"Oh, I decided not to do it."

"What a shock," says Jerry. "When do I get my dinner?"

Perplexed, Kramer looks at him. "There's no dinner. The bet's off. I could do it, but now I don't want to do it."

"That's the bet! Not that you could. That you wouldn't!"

We all make promises we intend to keep but then don't. Often, it's harmless, like building excessive levels. Other times, the stakes are much higher.

Some people might be able to get away with making grandiose statements in front of others. Perhaps it's common in some professions. However, as an emergency manager, your words matter in a crisis. People pay attention, even to the little promises. They'll make decisions based on what you say. Don't underestimate the compounding benefits of committing to doing this one thing well.

If you say you're going to do it, do it.

CHAPTER 10

Come Home

HOW TO BALANCE YOUR JOB AND YOUR LIFE

"My mission in life is not merely to survive, but to thrive; and to do so with some passion, some compassion, some humor, and some style."

—DR. MAYA ANGELOU

Montana Indian firefighters from the Confederated Salish Kootenai Tribes head home after battling a wildland fire in the Missionary Mountains. Photo by Andrea Booher/FEMA.

While I was deployed on a typhoon in the Western Pacific, my youngest child broke his arm in a hockey game. It was a bad fracture and snapped the bone. He was a star player, and now his season was over. I didn't *ask* permission from FEMA for a trip home. I *told* my boss I was taking emergency family leave. I flew from Guam to Tokyo, Tokyo to Houston, and Houston to Denver. The trip took forty hours. When I got home, I sat on the couch with him for five days watching sports and movies. Then I flew back to Guam.

I felt guilty about leaving the operation. I felt guilty about the burden I might have created by going home. When I got back to Guam, I felt even more guilty about not staying at home longer. You do your best.

FROM BEING IN AN OPERATION TO LEAVING IT

The emergency management lifestyle can be intoxicating. There's the camaraderie, discovering the wealth of local leadership in American cities, and the surprise of finding who steps up in a crisis—sometimes the most overlooked or eccentric. A kind of family also emerges when you work long hours together in an intense environment for an honorable mission.

All this can be incredibly addictive. Then it's time to come home. To survive and thrive in the disaster business, you need to learn how to arrive strong and go home well.

LEARN TO COMPROMISE

In emergency management, you will have to choose between your job and personal life. When do you ask your family to sacrifice so you can support the response? When will you decline a response assignment so you can help your family? This balancing act requires that you have an evaluation system for weighing priorities.

It also means accepting there aren't any perfect decisions, just better compromises. Toward the end of my father's life he needed at-home hospice care. FEMA arranged for me to work remotely while I took care of him at his condo in Sun Valley, Idaho, with my mom and siblings. My boss, Stacie Greff, set up a telework schedule so I wouldn't exhaust all my leave (telework was a relatively new concept at the time). Four hours a day of work and four hours a day off. When it looked like my dad's situation had temporarily stabilized, I left for a week to instruct at the Center for Domestic Preparedness in Anniston, Alabama, and then returned to his side.

You aren't just helping yourself when you come home well. You're enabling yourself to help coworkers when they face the same dilemma. You may see their needs more clearly than you see your own. I remember when one colleague told me her mom had stopped dialysis treatments and began in-home hospice. She struggled with what to do, overwhelmed at that moment to see clearly that her commitment to the disaster didn't matter. She needed to be with her mother at the end of her life. I told her to go home and that we would pay for her flight and get everything reassigned. She needed to hear that. It wasn't a decision she was able to make for herself.

EMBRACING THE CAUSE

You'll know whether this business is for you (or not) once you get your first disaster assignment. Either you will love it, or you won't. You may not expect how jarring it can be to go from working the disaster to stepping back into your home's front door. One day, you're briefing the president. The next day, you're burying your three-year-old daughter's turtle in the backyard. Guess which event is more important to your family.

The best crisis leaders do three things to manage this tug-of-war between an all-consuming career and maintaining a healthy personal life.

First, they recognize that it's an honor and a privilege to be an emergency manager. They don't blame their job for problems they might have in their personal life. What they do is essential. Their family respects them for that. They can look back on a professional life that encompassed incredible professional relationships, enviable memories, and accomplishments in the service of a worthy cause.

Second, successful crisis leaders recognize that their job takes a toll on physical, mental, and family health. As a new emergency manager, you may not know how much of yourself you give on every disaster assignment.

It's even harder for local responders who have to do their jobs while their home is damaged, their family has been evacuated, or their kids no longer have a school. If you are in this business, you need to consider this could happen. You may have to juggle doing your job to help the community with managing your own family's recovery at the same time.

When you are working a disaster in your hometown, you will

have to do all three: work the catastrophe, "demob" during the shift change, and come home, all on the same day. Then you'll do it all again the next day. Hometown disasters are the toughest, and those responders deserve our maximum support.

This leads to exceptional crisis leaders' third thing: managing their journey. It takes a long time to become valuable to your organization, which won't happen unless you keep your personal and professional lives together. Great emergency managers avoid burnout by staying fresh, positive, and healthy. They learn when to say no. They understand when to turn down assignments to go on a needed family vacation and, conversely, when to cancel a family vacation because the disaster needs them more.

Emergency management careers will suck you dry if you let them. Politicians see their jobs on the line and begin screaming for more help. Every new disaster becomes a priority. You get the call, and the next call, and another one. The thing is, once you get burned out, you'll be quickly replaced and soon forgotten. "Everyone is replaceable," John Swanson once told me.

This saying turned out to be prophetic. John took himself out of the lineup when he said his mental state was not good. He announced it at a staff meeting. John was pretty candid at a time when responders rarely discussed things like this. We were devastated. He was the king! We wondered how we would survive without him. Yet other people stepped up, and we did survive. John later came back for one more big disaster before retirement—and he crushed it. So don't ever feel guilty about stepping away.

THE THREE PHASES OF COMING HOME WELL

Responders who do a good job managing their personal life and their emergency management career pay attention to finding the right balance all the time. This means they focus on their well-being during the entire cycle of a disaster assignment: the deployed phase, the demobbing phase, and the coming home phase.

THE DEPLOYED PHASE

Responders help nobody if they burn out or get hurt. Worse, it can mean diverting resources to support the helpers, which means less for those impacted by the disaster. It's not a selfish act to take care of yourself on deployments. It supports the response operation, and the people affected.

Emergency managers recommend four pursuits that'll help you stay balanced.

1. a spiritual or an emotional support network
2. a creative outlet
3. an exercise routine
4. a sense of humor

Here are some examples of each.

A Spiritual or an Emotional Support Network

Ricardo "Zuni" Zuniga recommended connecting with your family every day. He said that each morning, his partner Debbie sent him an "all good at home" text, and each night he called her to check in. That was his emotional support. When Pat

Owens was mayor of Grand Forks after their flood, she visited with school children, who adored her, every time she needed to cheer her heart.

Other responders practice yoga or meditation or go to church. It's not unusual to find lapsed Catholics suddenly drawn back to Sunday mass when they're on a deployment.

A Creative Outlet

Creative outlets can include incorporating the arts in your emergency management portfolio or having a hobby. Fargo Mayor Dennis Walaker was a photographer and always seemed to have a camera hanging around his neck. Grand Forks' city attorney Howard Swanson was a fabulous cook. I heard Craig Fugate was a licensed amateur radio operator.

Other responders I know write fiction, paint, or play a musical instrument.

Ken Jordan spent his nights wood-carving beautiful statuettes that he would give away as gifts to relief workers. Longtime wildland firefighter Lynn Young was a member of the "Fiddlin Foresters," the official old-time string band of the US Forest Service.

An Exercise Routine

Many emergency management professionals also use exercise to keep them in shape physically and mentally during disasters. Tony Russell said he found it valuable to balance the mental side of emergency management—and its constant demand for analysis, decision-making, and communications—with a regular physical workout. Whether deployed to Bismarck or New Orleans, he always joined a local gym. Zuni rose every morning at five o'clock to swim. John Swanson would bring his bike on deployments. Gary Whitney fished. Andrea Booher hiked. Deanne Criswell and Steve Olsen both ran in local marathons. During the Big Four of '04 hurricane season in Florida, Bill Carwile regularly walked around a lake near his hotel.

A Sense of Humor

Don't underestimate the power of humor in a disaster response environment. I once gave a talk about my job at a high school, and I told some amusing stories. "Wow," said one student, "working disasters sounds like fun."

That took me aback for a second, but I had to be honest. "In a way, yes."

Inside the foxhole, humor on a disaster can make a point resonate, build team fellowship, and shed light on someone's fears. People are often most serious when they are joking. So, yes, there are many things on a disaster that make you laugh, which behavioral experts say is common within organizations that deal with death and destruction. That humor is a healthy antidote to stress and despair.

In a newspaper advertisement before his 1914 Imperial Trans-Antarctica Expedition, Sir Ernest Shackleton had this to say, which is an excellent example of setting realistic expectations:

"Men Wanted: For Hazardous Journey. Small Wages. Bitter Cold.

Long Months of Complete Darkness. Constant Danger. Safe Return Doubtful. Honour and Recognition in Event of Success."

Science also supports the power of laughter as a stress reliever. US Coast Guard Admiral Thad Allen took over the federal response to Hurricane Katrina in early September 2005, during the response's most trying and stressful time. The FEMA staff didn't know what to make of him, and many of us hadn't met him before. What's more, he is tall, barrel-chested, with the stern, imposing, no-nonsense presence of a big-time admiral, and he had everyone at FEMA on edge when he arrived.

We prepped a meeting room for Allen's first command brief with the federal agencies in one of our early encounters. As staff walked him through the room, explaining the layout and outlining the agenda, Admiral Allen looked around and picked up one of the cups and bottles of water that sat at each spot on the conference table.

"Where do you want to sit, sir?"

"Which cup will have the Jack Daniels in it?" he asked.

If Allen's goal was to get his new co-workers to find him approachable and have the confidence to bring issues to his attention, it worked.

When disaster colleagues reconnect and reminisce, even decades later, there's a lot of laughing. Crisis response adventures can be pretty wild, and the industry has more than a few endearing characters. Sometimes, these reunion stories become funnier the farther you age from the moment they occurred. Yet they offered humor and bonding benefits at the time, too.

THE DEMOBBING PHASE

When I first started more than three decades ago, responders denigrated mental health as "touchy-feely." There were limited services available, and people were looked at sideways for raising the subject or requesting help. One prevalent rumor suggested that you lose your security clearance by seeking counseling, which I heard when I started with FEMA.

The field has come a long way in valuing the mental health of emergency responders. Today, it is a required component of the response. I admire the new generation of emergency responders, who are much more open and honest about mental health issues. My deployment to Haiti required a visit with a crisis counselor before I left. I was surprised by how down I felt when it came time to go home. I guess I had survivor's guilt. This trained counselor really helped me and got me to a better place. I'm sure you'll take advantage of any resources available to you.

THE "BEING HOME" PHASE

Switching your brain off once you're home can be tricky, even after a successful "demobbing" stage. "It takes me a week or so to fully disengage once I come home," said Zuni.

Right away, though, avoid speaking in the frenetic, clipped language of disaster response at home where it's not needed.

For example, don't force your family to adopt crisis management organizational strategies and jargon. Someone said they instructed their family to use Incident Command System (ICS) concepts to plan their next vacation. If I had tried that, my family would have disowned me.

In my first several years in emergency management, I had difficulty turning off the tragedy after leaving. I would monitor the news coverage, check in with responders still there, and, worst of all, offer my unsolicited advice to the operation.

Eventually, I got better at shutting it down. I would leave the disaster in the rearview mirror and look ahead to what was going on at home. Speaking with crisis counselors helped me make this shift because it was a chance to get everything out before leaving the disaster.

HOW TO BE A BETTER COMPROMISER

My kids had a heart-to-heart talk with me. "You need to recognize how much your family sacrifices so you can do the job you love."

Working in emergency management means living two different lives. Your position and personal life may not intersect, but you will have to learn to manage both. It can feel like you have two families. You will love them both, but your real family should always come first. Never let your disaster job crowd out your responsibilities at home.

Putting your family first is not selfish; nor is it a career staller. The better you take care of your personal life, the better it is for the operation. You'll have fewer distractions and won't be dragging personal issues into the disaster.

This principle aims not to discourage you from embracing the cause, loving the adventure, and making a difference. It is a reminder to take care of yourself so that you can continue.

The business takes a toll on individuals. I've watched coworkers get divorced, lose their families, or pass away. The police even arrested one responder I knew well for murder (though he denied wrongdoing). I've gotten divorced.

I also often think about the times I've taken unnecessary risks—the adrenaline-fueled adventures, walking through sewage, breathing toxic air—that might come back to haunt me. It's not a surprise that too many of my mentors and former bosses died in their late sixties and early seventies.

And yet, I have never regretted answering the call for public service. Working with disaster survivors has taught me never to give up and to value the healing power of family. While every disaster assignment takes you on a different journey, they should all have the same destination at the end. Come home before you show up again.

Conclusion

During my first FEMA leadership assignment, I ran the federal response for a small flood in the upper Midwest. One night, strolling back to my hotel, I passed the large plate glass windows of a popular downtown restaurant not far from the state capitol.

I saw one of my employees, Carl, perched on a tall chair, back against the window, drinking scotch and playing blackjack. He was hard to miss, wearing his official agency jacket. Shoulder to shoulder, in large gold lettering, it said "FEMA." I stared, mesmerized by his lack of self-awareness, wondering what impression the coat in that environment might send.

The next day, I issued an all-hands policy memorandum titled Proper Use of Official Agency Clothing. "Agency-issued clothing is to be worn while conducting official agency business, but it should not be worn when off duty," I wrote. "FEMA employees need to be cognizant of our responsibility to present a professional image *at all times* while guests of the state."

I didn't name Carl, but he was the impetus for the memo. The purpose was to stop Carl from doing it again, and to stop anyone else from thinking it might be acceptable.

When handed a copy, Carl read it carefully. Then he crumpled the paper up, shook his head, and tossed it in the trash basket.

"This is so obvious," he said.

So much for me getting out a leadership message as a first-time leader.

Many aspiring emergency managers struggle early in their careers because they fall into the same trap as Carl. They ignore simple leadership principles merely because they seem obvious. They watch crisis leaders they admire and wonder what their secret is. They can't believe that the reason many have achieved so much and helped so many comes from having a core set of foundational principles those leaders bring with them to every disaster. It can't be that simple, the aspiring managers assume.

Yet it is.

"Don't be oblivious to the obvious" was one of the more helpful lessons I learned early in my emergency management career.

In my career, I often had the same reaction as Carl. It can't be that simple, I would think. These are obvious. Reading this book, you may have had the same thought.

The principles laid out here are apparent, but that doesn't make them automatic. It takes years of experience to master them.

You have to believe in them deep in your core. You have to practice these principles all the time.

I believe, though, that embracing these crisis leadership principles will give you the courage, compassion, and confidence to make better decisions, and transform you into someone others can count on when all hell breaks loose.

Try each of the ten principles. Show up. Step up. Think in threes. Own it. Promote the dog sitter. Be willing. Face failure. Talk straight. Follow up. Most importantly, come home.

After you try them, practice them. Internalize them. Bounce them off people you admire. You can revisit certain parts of the book if you find a particular principle helpful.

As you move forward in your career, you'll find yourself redefining or adding to this list based on your observations and experiences. That's great. It means you have seen the value of having core principles. And that's the point of this book. If I have convinced you of the need to have a set of foundational principles like all great leaders do, that will be good enough for me.

The ten principles are a reference point, a guiding star, and a way to make decisions when surrounded by chaos. They are by no means the definitive list. If you want to study more of the science, philosophy, history, or inspiration behind them, I have three suggestions.

First, the next time a crisis unfolds, watch for these principles in action or inaction. See how many you can spot. You also can apply this experiment to sporting events, which often provide an excellent example of will.

Second, try the same thing when you read a book. Biographies and historical fiction and nonfiction are good sources for examples of crisis leadership dilemmas and the importance of acting based on principles. A few books and authors have helped me and others understand crisis leadership principles. I suggest the following:

- Isaac's Storm: A Man, a Time, and the Deadliest Hurricane in History by Erik Larson
- No Ordinary Time: Franklin and Eleanor Roosevelt—The Home Front in World War II by Doris Kearns Goodwin (and her other books as well)
- Lonesome Dove by Larry McMurtry
- The Unthinkable: Who Survives When Disaster Strikes— and Why by Amanda Ripley
- Fire on the Mountain: The True Story of the South Canyon Fire by John N. Maclean (one of five nonfiction books he has written about wildland fire)
- The Great Influenza: The Story of the Deadliest Pandemic in History by John M. Barry
- It Worked For Me by Colin Powell (includes Powell's 13 Rules of Leadership)
- The Caine Mutiny by Herman Wouk
- For Whom the Bell Tolls by Ernest Hemingway
- Agility: How to Navigate the Unknown and Seize Opportunity in a World of Disruption by General Charles Jacoby and Leo Tillman
- The Tao of Leadership by John Heider

- Stronger in Broken Places: Nine Lessons for Turning Crisis Into Triumph by James Lee Witt and James Morgan
- Mountains Beyond Mountains: The Quest of Dr. Paul Farmer, A Man Who Would Cure the World by Tracy Kidder

Third, I would recommend making it a point to visit disaster memorials. In New York City, there's the 9/11 Memorial and Museum; and in Galveston, Texas, the 1900 Galveston Hurricane Museum. If you're driving on I-70 across western Colorado, stop and take a hike up the Storm King Mountain Memorial Trail near Glenwood Springs, built to honor the fourteen wildland firefighters who died battling the South Canyon Fire on July 6, 1994.

In New Orleans, you can go on a self-guided tour of different locations where the levees failed and see areas most severely impacted during Hurricane Katrina, including the Lower Ninth Ward. The Hurricane Katrina Memorial in New Orleans is located at 5056 Canal St. "Discreetly surrounded by cypress trees, it's the final resting place for the remains of the dead who were unclaimed or unidentified after the floodwaters receded," explains NOLA.com.

Similar tours and reflection experiences exist on the opposite border of the country in East Grand Forks, Minnesota, and Grand Forks, North Dakota, which rebuilt their communities following the 1997 Flood.

If this book has helped you, I'd love to know. Please send me a message through my website, www.edwardconley.com, or contact me via LinkedIn.

I provide personalized coaching and training services through my consulting firm, Conley Communications, for anyone interested. I don't work with the C-suite much. Plenty of top-notch crisis management consultants already do. Instead, I coach newcomers to the emergency management and homeland security fields.

Best wishes to you during your leadership journey. I'm pulling for you. The world needs a new generation of collaborative, compassionate, and courageous crisis leaders.

I will leave you with one final thought.

Above all, I want you to embrace the cause, love the adventure, and make a difference. If you do that, you will have a lifetime of memories. And what will make those memories memorable is that they won't be about disasters, chaos, and destruction. They'll be about the varying, sometimes messy, but undeniable resilience of people. The people you met, the people you worked with, the people who helped you, and the people you served. You'll never forget them. And they'll never forget you.

Stay safe.

Notes and Acknowledgments

Quotes have been drawn from personal interactions and experiences, interviews, books, television appearances, articles, and movies. The book also reflects my present recollection of experiences over time. I described events and conversations based on my memories of them. In certain instances, the names and identifying characteristics of some individuals have been changed, some events have been compressed, and some dialogue has been recreated.

I relied on my disaster notebooks for details regarding deployments, assignments, and observations. Statistics, disaster data, and after-action reports came from available online sources. Policies, executive orders, congressional testimony, and legislation are public records. I sourced data from scientific studies and credited dialogue from movies when referenced.

Source information for dialogue from the NBC sitcom *Seinfeld*:

1. *Seinfeld*, Season 5, episode 22, "The Opposite." Directed by Tom Chernos. Written by Larry David & Jerry Seinfeld and Andy Cowan, Aired May 19, 1994, on NBC.
2. *Seinfeld*, Season 2, episode 2, "The Pony Remark." Directed by Tom Chernos. Written by Larry David and Jerry Seinfeld. Aired January 30, 1991, on NBC.

Colin L. Powell's epigraph on optimism in chapter two also appeared on the US Department of State's website under "Former Secretary of State Powell's 13 Rules of Leadership." Dr. Doris Kearns Goodwin's quote on adversity—the chapter seven epigraph—appeared in a 2021 article published by masterclass. com. For the chapter nine epigraph, I quoted business executive and former American Express CEO Kenneth Chenault. In chapter 10, the quote from Dr. Maya Angelou is used with permission of Caged Bird Legacy, LLC, www.MayaAngelou.com.

All conclusions, criticism, kudos, and characterizations in the book are mine alone and should not be used to represent the beliefs of another individual or those of any organization or jurisdiction.

While *Promote the Dog Sitter* is a personal reflection on crisis leadership, many people contributed to it. The project gained momentum when several of my family's younger generation considered a public service career and asked me for advice. Starting with phone calls, emails, and face-to-face discussions, the final idea for the book began to emerge. Years later, I finished the project, and I wouldn't have been able to do so without the tremendous support I received.

Most important to me was the faith my family and friends

expressed during the process. I'm not the fastest writer, as they discovered. Yet not a single person close to me dismissed the project. They stuck with me, believed in the subject matter, and never seemed to have any doubt I'd get the book done. That was a huge boost and also a motivating factor. Special thanks to my wife Jiw; my children Jordan, Shea, and Jake; my mom; and champions Jim Chesnutt, Barb Sturner, Brett Hansard, Bart Green, Brian McGuire, and Darryl Madden. I'm eternally grateful as well to renowned documentary photographers, project enthusiasts, and great friends Andrea Booher and Michael Rieger.

Many people both mentioned and not mentioned in the book had a tremendous impact on shaping the thesis, sharpening lessons, and improving stories. I counted heavily on people I admired, trusted, and was proud to serve with during my FEMA years. Several of you shared personal stories with me. These stories helped me focus not only on the principles used during disasters, but also on why they matter and how responders demonstrate them, which is the crux of the book. I appreciate you all, and thank you for the time you spent with me.

Throughout my career, I've enjoyed great friendships and discussions on leadership. Many people have taken time over the years and in decades past to patiently and kindly listen to my ideas and share their own. I drew much from the wisdom of people-first leaders Lesli Rucker, Mary Hudak, Ken Jordan, Pete Bakersky, Bobbi Sanborn, Justo Hernandez, Scott Logan, Lacy Suiter, Tim Deal, Tony Russell, Rick Weiland, Steve Olsen, and Tom McCool. Thank you for your service to the nation and for being impactful role models for people like me.

I had the privilege of being around some incredible people

during my disaster years. Positive influencers in emergency management whom I tried my best to emulate include the incomparable James Lee Witt; the underappreciated R. David Paulison, who showed up and stepped up admirably to guide FEMA in the challenging years after Katrina; the unshakeable Dick Buck; the amazing and always supportive Josie Arcurio; and, going back to the beginning of my FEMA career, Dennis Kwiatowski, Deborah Hart, Bruce Baughman, and George Haddow. I appreciate what every one of you taught me, and also the opportunities you gave me.

I'm grateful to my first disaster bosses Ben Hendrickson and Donna Daniels; my early mentors Phil Cogan, Marvin Davis, Morrie Goodman, and Bri Rodriguez; North Dakota and Grand Forks stalwarts Pat Owens, Pete Haga, Howard and Debbie Swanson, brothers Charlie and Ken Vein, Major General Keith Bjerke, Doug Friez, Dennis Walaker, Hal Gersham, and Pat and Mary Richards; NATO cohorts Michael Tobin, David Klain, Irma Marsh, and Dan McElhinney; long-time colleagues and inspirational friends Ricardo Zuniga, Carol Hector-Harris, Doug Welty, Don Jacks, Debra Young, and Ken Higginbotham; wise sages Alan Dobson and Ron Sherman; the insightful Dr. Jacqueline McBride-Jones; unsung difference-makers Roger Jones, Lou Ramirez, Martin McNeese, and Scott Chamberlain; Wildland Fire Incident Commander Bob McCrea; and, especially, the through thick and thin crew Laurie Hassell, Jerry DeFelice, Brian Hvinden, Phil Wernisch, Megan Floyd, Cory Mitchell, Randy Welch, Justin Dombrowski, and Holly Stephens. I thought about all of you while I wrote this book.

Last, but certainly never least, thanks to everyone who took me over the finish line. There is nothing better than collaborating with good people who are wonderfully talented and willing to go above and beyond. Credit goes to Scribe's editing, publishing, cover design, and title superstars Chas, Nicole, Darnah, Michael, and Ami. Thanks also and bundles of appreciation to my New York-based project guides. Stephanie Siu was always available when I needed her incredible editing, beta feedback, and research contributions. And I was fortunate to connect with Carolyn Levin at Miller, Korzenik, Sommers, and Rayman, LLP., who was a pleasure to work with and provided expert legal counsel.

Finally, several people mentioned above and elsewhere in the book have passed on. I'm not alone in saying they're missed and haven't been forgotten. May they rest in peace.

About the Author

ED CONLEY served nearly three decades with FEMA, passionately leading teams around the globe in response to some of history's most significant disasters. He has also managed national incidents and international emergencies with the Coast Guard, Secret Service, Centers for Disease Control, and Department of State. Appointed as a US Liaison Representative with NATO, Ed traveled throughout Europe on emergency preparedness assignments. Before joining FEMA, he spent seven winters on the National Ski Patrol. An instructor with the Center for Domestic Preparedness and the National Emergency Training Center during his career, Ed resides in Seattle, Washington. Find more at Conley Communications (edwardconley.com).

CPSIA information can be obtained
at www.ICGtesting.com
Printed in the USA
LVHW100119071122
732515LV00005B/39/J